Time for Reflection

Text copyright © Ann Persson 2011
The author asserts the moral right to be identified as the author of this work

Published by
The Bible Reading Fellowship
15 The Chambers, Vineyard
Abingdon OX14 3FE
United Kingdom
Tel: +44 (0)1865 319700
Email: enquiries@brf.org.uk
Website: www.brf.org.uk
BRF is a Registered Charity

ISBN 978 1 84101 876 8
First published 2011
10 9 8 7 6 5 4 3 2 1 0

Acknowledgments
Unless otherwise stated, scripture quotations are taken from the New Revised Standard
Version of the Bible, Anglicised Edition, copyright © 1989, 1995 by the Division of Christian
Education of the National Council of the Churches of Christ in the United States of America,
and are used by permission • Scripture quotations taken from the Holy Bible, New
International Version, copyright © 1973, 1978, 1984, 1995 by International Bible Society.
Used by permission of Hodder & Stoughton Publishers, a member of the Hachette Livre UK
Group • Extracts from the Authorised Version of the Bible (The King James Bible), the rights
in which are vested in the Crown, are reproduced by permission of the Crown's Patentee,
Cambridge University Press • Scripture quotations from THE MESSAGE. Copyright © by
Eugene H. Peterson 1993, 1994, 1995. Used by permission of NavPress Publishing. • New
King James Version of the Bible copyright © 1979, 1980, 1982 by Thomas Nelson, Inc. All
rights reserved.

Extract from '*Ffrwydrad*' ('Explosion') by Gwilym R. Jones, taken from *Mae Gen i Lyn* (Barddas
Publications, 1986). Used by permission of the publisher • 'What can we bring…' by Kate
Compston, used by permission • 'God, food of the poor…', from *Páginas*, Lima, Peru, July
1987. Reprinted in *Latinamerica Press*, 5 November 1987 • 'Loving Father, we thank you for
feeding us…' from *Holy Week, Easter: Services and Prayers* is copyright © The Central Board of
Finance and is reproduced by permission of The Archbishops' Council, copyright@c-of-e.org.
uk • 'Blessed be God…' taken from *Easter Garden* by Nicola M. Slee. Copyright © 1990.
Used by permission of Zondervan. www.zondervan.com • 'Open the scriptures to me…',
from *Sacred Space: The Prayer Book 2007*, Jesuit Communication Centre, Ireland, used by
permission of Veritas • 'Risen Christ' and 'Spirit of truth' taken from *All Desires Known* by
Janet Morley, published by SPCK 1992. Used by permission of SPCK • 'A prayer for autumn
days', excerpted and adapted from *May I Have This Dance?* by Joyce Rupp, copyright 1992,
2007 by Ave Maria Press, Inc., PO Box 428, Notre Dame, IN 46556, www.avemariapress.com.
All rights reserved • 'O God, we thank you for the gift of years…' used by permission of the
Carmelites of Indianapolis • 'Thanksgiving' from *Waiting for the Kingsfisher* by Ann Lewin,
used by permission.

A catalogue record for this book is available from the British Library

Printed in Great Britain by CPI Bookmarque, Croydon

Time for Reflection

Ann Persson
Meditations to use through the year

*I dedicate this book to all those
with whom I have shared Quiet Days over many years.*

Contents

Introduction

There I was, on a warm day in May 1986, sitting alone in a small room at a convent in Oxfordshire. I was there for my first ever Quiet Day and not finding it very easy to settle into stillness. I am not sure who suggested the idea to me, but being a busy mother of four children and a 'people person', I was unused to having a day of quiet with no interruptions and no company but my own. The thought of it had seemed very appealing at the time, but now that I was there, I felt unsure of myself and even a bit guilty at walking away from all that there was to do at home. It took me a while (well, most of the day, in fact) to adjust to the silence. When it was time to leave, however, I was surprised to find that, far from feeling that I would not want to repeat the experience, I was mentally planning to return, maybe in six months' time.

So began my journey into discovering the value and refreshment that can be found in taking periodic quiet days. They act like punctuation marks that make sense of a piece of prose. Henri Nouwen describes taking time to be alone as 'lifting the drawbridge', which I find a helpful image. Although refreshing and restful, the aim is not so much for 'detox' or relaxation (although there are those benefits) but principally for taking time out to be with God.

Eight years earlier, my husband Paul and I had moved to Highmoor Hall, near Henley-on-Thames. We used our home as a facility to serve Christian leaders of all denominations. It became a place where they could meet together in groups or come individually to pray, plan and receive the vision and direction that God had for them in their ministry.

The house was built in 1661 in an area of great natural beauty. When we first arrived, we felt overwhelmed by looking after the six acres of garden, and at first we did little but try to maintain them as they were. Bit by bit, however, we gained confidence and began work to create a large pond, a 'secret garden' and secluded areas where people could sit with some privacy. When we had finished carving up the grounds, I became aware that God was saying, 'Now use them for me.' 'How, Lord?' was my reply. 'You can use them by offering Quiet Days for any who want to come and meet with me.' I can honestly say that it felt like an overwhelmingly clear directive, and this was long before Quiet Days had become popular. I was increasingly valuing my occasional days spent at the convent (they sometimes stretched to a retreat of three to four days), so, I thought, why not offer something similar at Highmoor Hall?

In the summer of 1988, we produced our first programme of led Quiet Days, with the title 'Time for Reflection', which has given rise to the title of this book. We were delighted by the response to our offering. The days had a simple framework, beginning at 10am and ending at 4pm, with lunch provided on individual trays so that there was no interruption to the silence. Three short sessions of input provided a theme and a springboard that the participants could develop in their times of quiet, if they wished to do so. We always made it clear that it was their day and they were free to follow God's agenda, not ours, but, if having a theme was helpful, then it was there for them to use. We had some very encouraging feedback and it was not long before the Time for Reflection days were offered throughout the year and not just in the summer.

Twenty-three years later, and eight years since we moved

from Highmoor Hall, I still have the privilege of leading Quiet Days, quite often for BRF, the publishers of this book. I am delighted to have the opportunity to pick up a few of the themes that I have used over the years, which you can dip into. You may like to take an hour or two or a longer period on your own, or you may choose to use one of the themes with a small group of people.

It was difficult to know which material to select, but as I thought about it, the word 'weaving' came into my mind. I remembered that three years before, Paul and I had woven a large willow circle—about four feet in diameter, as the focal point for an afternoon church service in praise of creation. It was transported to the top of a nearby hill where about 50 people gathered for a short introductory time of worship overlooking the plain of Oxford. Everyone was encouraged to thread wild flowers and foliage into the circle, which was then taken back down the hill and hung in the church for all to see. It looked beautiful. I see the contents of this book as a woven circle, too. There are three main strands— time, the Christian calendar, and the seasons of the natural year with their spiritual analogies. Inserted into this circle are other reflections that have a link to the main themes. For example, at Epiphany there is a reflection on the magi bearing gifts and coming to worship the infant king. I then insert an imaginative contemplation on a woman who also came bearing a gift to Jesus.

This is not a book to be read through, but a book that you can use when you have time for a period of quietness. I hope that you will find these reflections helpful in your Christian journey and an aid to prayer.

Ways into prayer

It is not easy to switch from activity to stillness; from noise to silence; from achieving to letting go; from doing to being in the presence of God. Personally, I cannot just decide to put on my 'contemplative hat' and settle into prayer. I find I need bridges from one state of mind to the other, and here are some of the bridges I find helpful.

- Making a drink
- Going for a short walk to wind down
- Having a visual focus—a candle, an icon, a painting, a poster or an object
- Playing restful, calm music
- Giving attention to my breathing, gradually deepening it and slowing the rhythm

The Chinese philosopher Lao-Tzu, who lived more than 2000 years ago, said:

> *Muddy water,*
> *let stand,*
> *becomes clear.*[1]

In the context of prayer, a time of stillness is needed to enable the sediment of our lives to settle so that we may have a true reflection of ourselves and of God within us.

Here are some suggestions to help you to come into stillness:

- Find somewhere quiet, where you will not be disturbed.
- Sit comfortably, relaxed and alert—straight back, hands in your lap, shoulders easy, head up, comfortably supported by your neck. Give your weight to the ground, open and soften your upper body, relax your face muscles and let any unwanted tension drain away.
- Be aware of the rhythm of your breathing. Then slow it down just a little and have a sense of it dropping from chest level to lower down the spine and settling in the abdominal area—deep, easy breathing, like lazy waves breaking on the shore and receding.
- When you notice your mind wandering, gently return to following your breath.
- It may help to breathe into a name or phrase over and over again, for example, 'Abba, Father'; 'Jesus, Lord'; 'Peace, be still'—whatever you choose.

Coming to God

This is another way of quietening your inner noise and bringing you into a sense of God's presence.

- As you sit comfortably, gather as many thoughts as you can that are buzzing around in your head. When you have identified them, pull one dominant thought or concern to the fore, acknowledge it and then, when you are ready, deliberately give that thought to God and let it go. Breathe more slowly and let your mind be at rest.
- Your focus then drops to the chest area, where anxieties or excitement are usually felt. Gather together what concerns you, what is making you feel anxious or excited. Identify a

dominant feeling, acknowledge it and, when you are ready, as before, give it to God. Take a long outgoing breath as you let it slide away. Be at peace and breathe easily.

- Descend to the area of your abdomen and down to gut level. Here you can focus on your longings, hopes, desires and fears. It may take a little longer to get in touch with what is going on in these deeper reaches of yourself. Again, try to identify which is the dominant emotion, acknowledge it and, when you feel ready, surrender it to God so that you may create space for him. Your breathing will now be done lower in your body, so that your chest walls will barely be moving. With each breath out, you descend lower and lower.

- Finally, you descend to the very ground of your being. Become aware of your longing for God. After a while, let go even of that longing until there is simply you and God. No words are needed, no thoughts or feelings: just be with him, rest in him, staying there for as long as you want, at peace.

When you are ready, slowly return through the gut level, the chest area and back to your mind. Open your eyes, if you have closed them, and move out in communion with God.

Ways of praying

Because we are people with a variety of personalities, it is inevitable that some ways of praying will be helpful to one type of personality and not to another. Below are some suggestions that you may find helpful, depending on the sort of person you are.

11

Lectio divina or 'holy reading' is a way of meditating on the Bible. I am told that centuries ago, before Bibles were widely available, the abbot of a monastery would gather his monks together and read to them the Bible passage set for the day. He would read it three times and the brothers were encouraged to listen attentively and choose a phrase to remember. They would then go about their daily work in the garden, in the kitchen, in the infirmary, wherever and whatever they were doing, and through the day they would meditate on the phrase they had chosen. Rather like sucking a boiled sweet, they would draw out its meaning for themselves.

You might like to try something similar:

- Choose a passage from the Bible and begin to read it very slowly, as if it were addressed to you. A few verses from Psalm 103 would be a good place to start.
- Stop when a phrase captures your attention. Maybe it touches you in some way, attracts or even disturbs you. It is like catching a falling leaf. Hold on to it.
- Repeat the phrase slowly over and over again, taking its meaning into you. Let it sink in slowly. What does it have to say to you? Why do you think it caught your attention? Where is the connection for you?
- Move into prayer, expressing the thoughts and feelings that have spontaneously arisen in you.
- Let your mind be at rest and your heart open to the love and peace of God. When you are ready, carry on with reading the next bit of the passage.
- Follow the example of the monks and return to your phrase or phrases during the day.

The Ignatian way

This is a way of praying devised by St Ignatius of Loyola, the Spanish founder of the Jesuits, who lived from 1491 to 1556. It uses the imagination to bring Gospel scenes into the present moment and is an approach to prayer that engages both the senses and the emotions.

- Before your prayer time begins, select a Gospel passage. Some passages that lend themselves to this form of prayer are:
  * Luke 2:1–20 ....The birth of Jesus
  * Matthew 3:13–17........................ The baptism of Christ
  * John 2:1–12.......................... The wedding feast at Cana
  * John 1:35–51.....................The call of the first disciples
  * John 4:1–42..............................The woman at the well
  * Luke 10:38–42 .... At the home of Mary and Martha
  * Matthew 14:22–33.......................Jesus walks on water
  * Luke 7:36–50 ....Jesus anointed by a woman
  * Mark 10:46–52 .... The healing of blind Bartimaeus
  * John 13:1–17................Jesus washes the disciples' feet
  * John 20:10–18..........Jesus appears to Mary Magdalene
  * John 21:1–19............................ Breakfast on the beach

- Spend some moments settling down and finding a comfortable position. Ask God to speak to you through the passage that you have chosen.

- Read the verses slowly and carefully, a few times over. Then put the Bible aside.

- Bring the scene to life in your imagination. What can you see, smell, hear, feel, even taste?

- Now enter the scene, choosing to be whoever you want—a disciple, a bystander, a blind or sick person.
- Let the events of the story unfold. Don't try to control or analyse them. Let whatever happens happen.
- Listen to any words spoken by Jesus. Perhaps they are addressed to you? Let yourself respond as feelings arise in you.
- When you have come to the end of the encounter, take some time to rest.
- It is helpful to write down any emotions, moods or reactions that were part of your experience. Take them to Jesus in prayer. What does he want to say to you? How do you want to respond?

Praying with icons

Icons were never intended as objects to be worshipped but simply as 'windows on to the divine'. They are doorways into stillness and communion with God, who is love.

The word 'icon' comes from the Greek *eikon* and means 'image', and, although they are generally associated with the Orthodox Church, in recent years icons have become increasingly popular with Christians of all backgrounds.

Different icons have different meanings and 'moods'. For example, Christ Pantocrator (Almighty or Ruler of the Universe) from St Catherine's Monastery in the Sinai desert looks at you with blessing and points to the Holy Scriptures. The icon of the Virgin of Vladimir shows the tenderness between Mary and Jesus. She points to her son but her eyes are sorrowful as she anticipates his suffering. Rublev's icon of the Trinity contains many layers of meaning. (I have written a book, *The Circle of Love*, about praying with this icon.)

14

Icons are available from some Christian bookshops or websites, or you can simply search for icons online. Many of us were taught to pray with our eyes closed, but praying with an icon involves keeping your eyes open and taking into your heart what the image communicates. This is prayer without words, with the aim of resting in God's presence. As you pray, cultivate an inner attitude of listening and allow God to speak to you and reassure you of his love.

Taking a prayer walk

'Most people come here to walk their dogs. Me, I have come to walk my soul.' So wrote my friend, Joanna Tulloch, after returning from a morning stroll near her home.

Sometimes it is hard to settle into prayer because we feel restless or a bit 'wound up'. This is when a leisurely walk with God can help. Firstly, if your mind is in overdrive, you can let your thoughts wander where they will. Gradually, let your pace slacken and your mind quieten down. When you are ready, focus on each of your senses in turn, starting with sight. What can you see above you, in the distance, around you or on the ground? Gently turn your thoughts into a prayer of praise, thanksgiving or intercession.

You can then give your attention to what you hear, smell and touch, and let that lead you into prayer. Be aware, too, of the ground beneath your feet. You are walking on the crust of our molten planet. Walk gently on God's earth. If possible, before returning, find somewhere to sit for a few minutes and know yourself to be in communion with God the Creator, who is also your loving Father.

Journalling

For some people, the act of writing or drawing concentrates the mind, and the practice of keeping a journal is another spiritual discipline that has recently grown in popularity. Your journal can be a place where you are free to express your inmost thoughts, feelings, questions, doubts or confusion, all of which can lead into prayer. Or you can take a Bible passage and, instead of quietly meditating on it and perhaps battling with straying thoughts and distractions, write down your findings and how they relate to issues that you might be facing at the time.

I hope you have found at least one of these suggestions helpful. We turn now to the reflections themselves.

What time is it?

As a visual focus, I suggest a clock or a watch and a calendar.

The theme of time weaves its way through this book, so where better to begin than by asking the question, 'What time is it?' I suspect that most of you will glance at your watch or a clock several times in the day—perhaps in disbelief in the morning when you have to get up, especially in winter; maybe nervously before an appointment; to judge when a meal is cooked or to turn on the television for the news or a favourite programme.

In countries that emphasise the importance of keeping track of time, it is amazing how much we internalise the awareness of it. I can wake up in the middle of the night and find that I can often guess the time instinctively, with no reference points to help me. Three years ago, I took a fortnight's retreat in a small cottage in a remote area of Wales. I had no car, no radio, no television, no telephone, and I decided to take off my watch, so that I was not controlled by time. It was very freeing, and yet, on the few occasions when I looked at my watch in its hiding place, I was not surprised to find that what I thought might be the time was indeed right to within a quarter of an hour or so. Time was in my system.

There is a passage in Ecclesiastes 3:1–8 about time. Although the author may have been King Solomon, the name given is the Teacher. As an old man, he looks at life with a long perspective, concluding at the end of his book that our efforts on earth are meaningless apart from God. His reflections on time are very thought-provoking:

For everything there is a season,
and a time for every matter under heaven:
a time to be born, and a time to die;
a time to plant, and a time to pluck up what is planted;
a time to kill, and a time to heal;
a time to break down, and a time to build up;
a time to weep, and a time to laugh;
a time to mourn, and a time to dance;
a time to throw away stones, and a time to gather stones together;
a time to embrace, and a time to refrain from embracing;
a time to seek, and a time to lose;
a time to keep, and a time to throw away;
a time to tear, and a time to sew;
a time to keep silence, and a time to speak;
a time to love, and a time to hate,
a time for war, and a time for peace.

My grandparents lived in a stone house in the Yorkshire Dales. In the hall stood an imposing grandfather clock, which had a distinctive tick-tock, tick-tock sound. I remember, as a young girl, standing in front of it, mesmerised by its steady, relentless tick-tock. I would wait for the sonorous chimes each quarter of an hour.

Sometimes, I would sit on the stairs and just listen to it, fascinated, waiting for the hour to be struck. Then it would resume its regular tick-tock and I would think of the minutes slipping by. Spend a moment looking at your watch or clock and be aware of the seconds and the minutes ticking by— time that will never come again.

When I read the passage from Ecclesiastes above, it makes me think of the rhythm of a ticking clock, although the writer would not have known about clocks, of course. He would have told the time by the sun and by the position and length of the shadow thrown by a pole on a flat surface. I find that there is a gentle ebb and flow to the pattern of the verses, which creates a sense of inevitability about the cycle of life experiences.

Pause for reflection

Read the passage again slowly. Are there any words that resonate with you? It would be helpful to write them down, together with the ways in which they link to your life experience.

Do you want to move from one state of being to another—for example, from keeping silent to speaking up or the other way round?

Take as much time as you need to think and pray through the issues that come to mind.

Two kinds of time

The English language has only one word for 'time' but the ancient Greeks understood that time was too complex to be contained in one word, so they had two: *chronos* and *kairos*.

Chronos time

Chronos time is what we know as chronological time and it is what we live with on a daily basis. There is morning, noon and night; spring, summer, autumn and winter; beginning, middle and end.

Chronos time is measured in units, so there are 60 seconds in a minute, 60 minutes in an hour and 24 hours in a day, which is the length of time that the earth takes to rotate on its axis. There are twelve months, or 365 or 366 days in a year, which is the measure of the earth's orbit around the sun—and so it goes on and on and on.

We use clocks to tell the time. We strap small clocks to our wrists and call them 'watches', because with them we can watch *chronos* time coming and going. Time often seems to be more of a taskmaster than a friend, as there is rarely enough of it. We can feel stressed as we race the clock, going about our regular activities. *Chronos* time is what we use to schedule appointments: 'I'll meet you at 3 o'clock.' The diary or calendar becomes an important accessory as we keep track of what we have planned to do in the time ahead.

If you have a calendar beside you, look ahead to appointments and arrangements that you have entered on it. How far ahead are you planning? Are there gaps for rest and recreation?

Chronos time is time on the move, as the future passes through the present and so becomes the past. It is something over which we have no control. Each human being has exactly the same number of hours and minutes every day. Rich people cannot buy more hours. Scientists cannot invent new minutes. There is no one powerful enough to stop the march of time. You cannot save time to spend it on another day, but, no matter how much time you have wasted in the past, you still have an entire tomorrow. Each new day is like a fresh, blank sheet for you to write on.

None of us knows when our time will be up, when life on earth will come to an end. Time is to be treated as a precious gift from God and used carefully.

The psalmist writes, 'Teach us to count our days that we may gain a wise heart' (Psalm 90:12).

For reflection

If you think of your life in terms of a clock, what time would it show now?

- How do you feel about this time?
- What is good about this time?
- Is there something challenging about this time?
- Is there anything you want to say to God about this time?

This amusing prose-poem has been attributed to various people, including Nadine Stair, an 85-year-old woman from Kentucky, USA:

If I had my life to live over, I'd dare to make more mistakes next time. I'd relax, I would limber up. I would be sillier than I have been this trip. I would take fewer things seriously. I would take more chances. I would climb more mountains and swim more rivers. I would eat more ice cream and less beans. I would perhaps have more actual troubles, but I'd have fewer imaginary ones.

You see, I'm one of those people who lived sensibly and sanely, hour after hour, day after day. Oh, I've had my moments, and if I had to do it over again, I'd have more of them. In fact, I'd try to have nothing else—just moments, one after another, instead of living so many years ahead of each day. I've been one of those persons who never goes anywhere without a thermometer, a hot water bottle, a raincoat and a parachute. If I had to do it again, I would travel lighter than I have.

If I had my life to live over, I would start barefoot earlier in the spring and stay that way later in the fall. I would go to more dances. I would ride more merry-go-rounds. I would pick more daisies.

As you look back over your life, are there any instances in which you would have chosen to use your time differently? You may like to complete this sentence:

If I had the opportunity to live my life over again, I would...

What might this suggest about how you choose to use the future?

Prayer

I trust in you, O Lord; I say, 'You are my God.' My times are in your hand. (Psalm 31:14–15)

Kairos time

Kairos time might be roughly translated 'the right moment'— a time that has significance or one in which we feel completely absorbed, so that we lose track of *chronos* time. We are utterly caught up in the moment, whether it is in prayer, a creative process, listening to a piece of music or captured by a sight in nature. Unlike *chronos* time, the emphasis is on quality rather than quantity. These are special moments that have extra meaning and are probably those that we will recall in later life. We say, 'I'll never forget when…'

One such moment was on 1 December 1955, when Rosa Parks, an African-American woman, tired after a day's work, sat down on a bus in Montgomery, Alabama. When asked by the bus driver to give up her seat to make room for a white passenger, she simply said, 'No.' She was tired of giving way and she had had enough of racial discrimination. Her action sparked the Montgomery bus boycott and became an important symbol of the modern civil rights movement. She worked with Martin Luther King, helping to launch him to national prominence in the civil rights movement. That was a *kairos* moment. It was the right time.

Kairos can also be described as God's time; the time of God's choosing; a time when God breaks through and changes the course of human history. Through the birth of Jesus, God's *kairos* time entered the *chronos* time of this world. Paul writes, 'But when the fullness of time had come, God sent his Son, born of a woman, born under the law… so that we might receive adoption as children (Galatians 4:4–5).

The death of Jesus, his resurrection and ascension, the day of Pentecost and Saul's conversion on the road to Damascus were all *kairos* moments, as will be the promised second coming of Jesus Christ.

As you think over your life's journey, you will recognise significant times—*kairos* moments. I can think of one particular time for me and my husband. For 26 years, we had used our home as a retreat house and we had built an arts and resource centre in the garden. Many people came to enjoy the facilities. We were very happy there and, although we were getting older (70 and 65 years old), we could have continued for a few more years. Yet we had a growing sense—not a flash—that it was God's time for us to begin to pack up and leave. Had we not done so, the Christian couple who now live there would not have bought it and further developed it, as they have, for God's purposes.

Several people asked us if we were upset or sad at leaving, but my experience is that, when it is *kairos* time, God's right time, if we go with it he will also take care of our emotions. And so it has been.

For reflection
As you look back on your life, can you detect the *kairos* moments?

- Times that were significant for you, maybe pivotal moments?
- Times when you were completely absorbed, unaware of 'ticking' time?
- Times when you knew that the Spirit of God was nudging you to take some course of action?

Thinking of time as sacred, do you need to make any changes in your priorities and in your use of it? Maybe you can think about setting limits; being aware of which activities drain you and which excite and nurture you; perhaps managing your time better so that you can allow for more free-flowing time, or focusing more on 'living the moment'.

A prayer

Jesus, Lord of time, hold us in your eternity.
Jesus, who lived in time, travel with us moment by moment.
Jesus, Lord of tomorrow, draw us into your future. Amen

The God who comes

Advent, which falls at the end of November or the very beginning of December, is a special time of preparation as we draw near to celebrating the birth of Jesus Christ, the Son of God. This meditation will be in three parts:

- Christ came
- Christ comes
- Christ will come again

You will need a Bible, and you might like to light a candle before you start, as a symbol that Jesus Christ is the light of the world.

Part 1: Christ came

God is a self-revealing, self-communicating, self-giving God. He is totally committed to us and desires to make himself known to us. Unbreakable threads of his love and mercy are woven throughout human history.

At creation, God saw all that he had made and that it was very good, but disobedience and independence damaged and broke the relationship between humankind and God.

In his mercy, God chose Abraham to father his chosen people. They would be the womb-community from whom would issue the promised Messiah.

He called Moses to be the law-giver and to lead his people out of bondage in Egypt towards the promised land. He instructed Moses to make a tabernacle that would be a tent of meeting and in it to place the ark of the covenant, which would be a symbol of God's presence: 'Have [the Israelites] make me a sanctuary, so that I may dwell among them' (Exodus 25:8).

God was faithful and the children of Israel inhabited the land that was promised to them. The ark was eventually taken to Jerusalem at the command of King David. His son Solomon was instructed by God to build a temple and the ark was placed in the Holy of Holies there.

The people of Israel were wayward, though, and began to worship the gods of their pagan neighbours and to intermarry with pagans. God's love and commitment prompted him to plead with his people through the prophets whom he raised up, urging them to leave their sinful ways, to turn their backs on idolatry and back to him, the one true God. Like the tide of the sea, they turned towards him but then turned away again—not once but many times. But every time they repented and turned back to God, he had mercy on them and forgave them.

The love that burned in the heart of the Trinity and the desire to be in relationship with humankind led to a truly amazing, even scandalous plan. God himself would become human, taking on our nature and the limitations of the human condition so that he could be touched, heard, seen and loved; so that our brokenness could be healed and we could be brought into a new and living relationship with God the Father, God the Son and God the Holy Spirit.

At the right time, God chose a young girl, possibly aged only about 16. Her name was Mary from Nazareth. She would be God's ark, his temple, a safe enclosure, a womb in which to be conceived and to develop and grow towards the moment of birth. It was the courtesy of God that asked Mary's permission, and he only acted on her 'Yes': 'Then Mary said, "Here am I, the servant of the Lord; let it be with me according to your word"' (Luke 1:38). I am sure there was a Hallelujah chorus in heaven as those words were uttered. I can almost see the angels straining to hear her response!

For the nine months of Jesus' unborn life, Mary was like the new ark of the covenant, the place of God's dwelling with his people. God revealed himself to us through Jesus; God communicated himself to us through Jesus; God gave himself to us through Jesus. We are familiar with the facts but, when you stop to think about it, it is quite breath-taking.

As to the manner of his coming, it was in utter simplicity, possibly in poverty. The tiny infant was endangered in many ways. His parents had to make a 70-mile journey while Mary was heavily pregnant; she would not have her mother and other trusted women to help her at the birth, and an unhygienic stable or cave were not the surroundings we would choose for a birth today. God had become one of us.

His life continued in the same humble way. For his first three years he was a refugee in Egypt and then grew up in the simple hilltop village of Nazareth, eventually working alongside Joseph as a carpenter. God became a 'chippie'.

Jesus moved only at his Father's initiative, and so he waited for 30 years before starting his servant ministry. He healed, taught, cared for people, confronted hypocrites, slept rough and walked tirelessly from place to place. Many believed in him and the message he brought about the kingdom of God. But he was also misrepresented, criticised, beaten and finally put to death:

Let the same mind be in you that was in Christ Jesus, who, although he was in the form of God, did not regard equality with God as something to be exploited, but emptied himself, taking the form of a slave, being born in human likeness. And being found in human form, he humbled himself and became obedient to the point of death—even death on a cross. (Philippians 2:5–8)

But for Jesus, death was not the end. Just as he had promised, on the third day he was resurrected, triumphantly defeating death:

Therefore God also highly exalted him and gave him the name that is above every name, so that at the name of Jesus every knee should bend, in heaven and on earth and under the earth, and every tongue should confess that Jesus Christ is Lord, to the glory of God the Father. (Philippians 2:9–11)

The heart of God is love, but it was costly. He did not take the easy way when he came.

For reflection
Read through the following passages slowly and choose one to meditate on, opening your heart and mind to its message.

Jesus,
what made you so small?
Love! [1]

Wonder of all wonders in one sight!
Eternity shut in a span.
Summer in winter, Day in night,
Heaven in earth and God in man.
Great little one! Whose all-embracing birth
Lifts earth to heaven, stoops heav'n to earth.[2]

Through Jesus, our greatest treasure,
came an explosion of true love.
He shattered the splendid walls
of the proud fortresses of the world's great ones.
He put his hand in the hand of the weak
and brought peace to humble dwellings.[3]

This is how God showed his love among us: he sent his one and only Son into the world that we might live through him. This is love: not that we loved God, but that he loved us and sent his Son as an atoning sacrifice for our sins. (1 John 4:9–10, NIV)

Part 2: Christ comes

This is a time of year that has its own unique festive character, with twinkling lights and decorations, wrapping paper and secrets, smells of pine and spice, quantities of food and drink to celebrate the season. Hopefully, at the heart of it all is love—love in the family and love among friends—because our human love is a pale reflection of the burning love that God has for us, love that would send his own beloved Son to live among us.

Christ's coming is threefold. He came; he comes; he will come again. Two of his comings are clearly visible but the third is not.

In his first coming, he was seen by the shepherds, the magi and others in the town of Bethlehem. He was seen as a newborn baby who grew into manhood, living out his life among ordinary folk.

In his final coming, we read, 'every eye will see him' (Revelation 1:7) and, as Paul writes, 'we will see face to face' (1 Corinthians 13:12).

But the coming that lies between these two is hidden, and only those who are open to his Spirit will recognise his presence within themselves, in others and around them. He promised to come to us, for on the eve of his crucifixion he said to his disciples, 'I will not leave you orphaned; I am coming to you' (John 14:18). This promise was fulfilled on the day of Pentecost, when the Holy Spirit came upon the disciples who were gathered together in Jerusalem, as he continues to come to all those who believe in Jesus Christ.

In his first coming, Christ came in human flesh, in weakness and with limitations.

In his intermediate coming, in the present, he comes in Spirit, in power and in love.

In his final coming, he will be seen in glory and majesty.

In what ways does he come to us?

He came, the first time, in such an ordinary, lowly way, living in the hurly-burly, the ups and downs of life. Therefore, he comes to us now in the ordinariness of our lives. When I am leading a Quiet Day on this theme, I like to use as a

visual aid a table laden with tokens of the stuff of our lives—
files, laptops, an iron, cereal packet, trainers, mobile phone,
gardening tools, books and newspapers, a kettle, a coffee
mug and other things. Among all the clobber I place a tall
lit candle to symbolise the fact that Christ is with us by his
Spirit in all that we do and wherever we are. For in the frail
envelope of our bodies we contain the Spirit of God. Like
Mary, we have become Christ-bearers.

As Paul wrote to the Christians in Corinth, 'Do you not
know that you are God's temple and that God's Spirit dwells
in you?' (1 Corinthians 3:16).

How do we recognise his coming?

He comes to us through the Eucharist, Holy Communion,
the Lord's Supper—whatever name you choose to give it.

He reveals himself to us through scripture.

He comes close to us in prayer as we draw close to him
and listen to him, whether we are aware of him or not. He
speaks into our silence and he speaks through the prayers of
others.

He comes among us as we gather together to worship him,
and he comes as we work together.

We discover him through each other, in words and
actions, in celebration and sorrow, in love, repentance and
forgiveness.

He comes in the guise of the needy, the poor, the sick, the
deprived, the dying.

He inspires us through nature—its wildness and its
gentle beauty; through its serenity, colour, form, movement
and minute detail. He comes through wildlife and through
domesticated animals—our pets.

He moves us in music and joins us in creativity.

He opens our eyes through art and meets us in books.

He whispers into our imagination and visits us in dreams.

He is present in laughter and in tears.

He comes in little things, so that, as Evelyn Underhill writes, 'he might pass the low lintel of the human heart'.[4] He finds little ways of touching us and of letting us know that he is there.

He disturbs us—he is the wild God that we try to tame—but he also comforts us.

He challenges us; he protects us.

He anoints us for specific acts of service.

He stills us; he energises us.

He heals us; he guides us.

He forgives us.

He comes so often as the God of surprises.

We have a part to play

Our part is to train our senses so that we become more aware of him, responding to his nods and nudges, his checks and his inspiration; so that we don't fall into the trap that John writes about in the prologue to his Gospel: 'He came to what was his own, and his own people did not accept him' (John 1:11). If we knew how to listen to God, if we knew how to look around us, our whole life would become prayer. We are to be like satellite dishes, open and angled towards him so that we pick up the signals he wants to give us.

His coming at Bethlehem shows that he is one who desires to be among us, not closeted away. He is Emmanuel—God with us—now, today, always.

For reflection

If we knew how to look at life through God's eyes, we should see it as innumerable tokens of love of the Creator seeking the love of his creatures. The Father has put us into the world, not to walk through it with lowered eyes, but to search for him through things, events and people. Everything must reveal God to us. Long prayers are not needed in order to smile at Christ in the smallest details of daily life.[5]

Our God is a God who gives himself; that is his glory. From all eternity he dwells in unapproachable light, yet he comes to find us, to call us, to offer his friendship and ask for ours. His Trinitarian glory is self-giving love, and it overflows, as is the way with love; so he is glorified not by remaining inaccessible but by self-communication. This is what revelation is: God speaking, not to present us with a list of truths we must believe or rules we must obey, but to utter himself.[6]

Questions

- In what ways have you experienced God coming to you?
- How has he made himself known and what has been your response?
- In the light of the following quote, is there any house-keeping to be done?

Brothers and sisters, it is now the season of the Lord's coming, and we must use the time to prepare ourselves by some spiritual devotion. We must strive to enter the house of our hearts, open the windows, and notice what is seemly

and what is unseemly in our house. We must brush away
cobwebs, sweep the floors, clear out the dust and dirt, straw
the clean floors with freshly gathered rushes, fragrant herbs
and sweet-smelling flowers.[7]

Prayer

O Lord,
you are around us,
above us, beneath us,
before us, behind us.
By your Spirit
you live within us.

O Lord,
sharpen our minds,
open our hearts,
touch our souls
that we might recognise you
and the ways in which you come to us.

O Lord,
for all the signs of your presence,
we give you thanks. Amen

Part 3: Christ will come again

Reflect on how Luke describes the ascension of Jesus to his
Father's presence, after the resurrection:

While [Jesus] was going and [the disciples] were gazing up towards
heaven, suddenly two men in white robes stood by them. They said,

'Men of Galilee, why do you stand looking up towards heaven? This Jesus, who has been taken up from you into heaven, will come in the same way as you saw him go into heaven.' (Acts 1:10–11)

At his first coming, he was wrapped in swaddling cloths and laid in a manger.

At his final coming, he will be clothed in light as in a garment.

At his first coming, he endured the cross, despising the shame.

At his final coming, he will be exalted in majesty.

At his first coming, only a few saw him.

At his final coming, every eye will see him.

In between these two comings there is the secret coming of the Spirit in the lives of all those who receive him.

Unlike the two former comings, the final coming is outside our experience. It will transcend all events in space and time that have ever been experienced, and so a full description is impossible.

We have a glimpse of the risen glorified Jesus in John's vision when, as an old man, he was living on the island of Patmos. In Revelation 1:9–18 we read of his vision of Christ with shining face, snow-white hair, flaming eyes, feet like burnished bronze and with a voice like the sound of a mighty waterfall.

Jesus himself told his disciples about his return and the end of the age. In Matthew 24:29–31 we read that the sun, moon and stars will be 'shaken' and this will herald the coming of Christ 'on the clouds' with great power and glory, when he will be seen by all the people of the world.

In 1 Thessalonians 4:16–18, Paul writes what he has been told about the event. He prefaces his description with 'According to the Lord's word' (v. 15, NIV). The doctrine he unfolds here is not recorded in the Gospels, so it was either a direct revelation to Paul or something that Jesus said, which was passed on orally but not written down.

There will be a rapturous moment when we finally meet God, and then will come the judgment. But we need not fear. That judgment is entrusted to the same Jesus who gave his life for us, motivated by love, and after it he will establish the kingdom of God for all eternity. As is declared in the Nicene Creed, 'He shall come again in glory to judge the living and the dead, and his kingdom shall have no end.'

In his first coming, Jesus of Nazareth did not even come close to fulfilling some of the soaring predictions of the prophets or the message of the angels announcing his birth: 'Glory to God in the highest, and on earth peace, good will toward men' (Luke 2:14, KJV). He was limited to Palestine. He came as the suffering servant of Isaiah 53. As John the Baptist recognised, he came as the Lamb of God who takes away the sin of the world, and there is still unrest in the world.

At his second coming, though, he will indeed establish peace on earth and glory to God. In the words of Handel's 'Hallelujah' chorus (taken from Revelation 19:6; 11:15 and 19:16), we can join the song of heaven:

Hallelujah! for the Lord God Omnipotent reigneth.
The kingdom of this world
is become the kingdom of our Lord

and of his Christ;
and he shall reign for ever and ever.
King of kings and Lord of lords. Hallelujah!
MESSIAH, G.F. HANDEL

But when will all this take place?

Jesus said in answer to that question, 'But about that day or hour no one knows, not even the angels in heaven, nor the Son, but only the Father' (Matthew 24:36, NIV). He went on to say, 'Therefore you also must be ready, for the Son of Man is coming at an unexpected hour' (v. 44).

But he gave us signs to look for, and you might agree that the list sounds a bit familiar: wars, famines, plagues (pandemics), earthquakes, changes in the sky, false Messiahs, side-lining and persecution of Christians, and lawlessness.

We are, I think, living in apocalyptic times. Before we destroy our beautiful planet home, we can say with the writer of the book of Revelation, 'Amen. Come, Lord Jesus!' (22:20).

For reflection

Let your imagination lead you into wonder at the promise of the return of Christ. Imagine the sounds, the light and colour and movement. How would you want to describe the experience? What might be your response?

You may like to capture your thoughts in a piece of writing or in art.

This is how one hymn writer envisaged the scene:

I cannot tell how He will win the nations,
How he will claim His earthly heritage,
How satisfy the needs and aspirations
Of east and west, of sinner and of sage,
But this I know, all flesh shall see his glory,
And he shall reap the harvest He has sown,
And some glad day His sun shall shine in splendour
When He, the Saviour, Saviour of the world is known.

I cannot tell how all the lands will worship,
When at His bidding, every storm is stilled,
Or who can say how great the jubilation
When all the hearts of men with love are filled.
But this I know, the skies will thrill with rapture
And myriad, myriad human voices sing,
And earth to heaven, and heaven to earth will answer:
At last the Saviour, Saviour of the world, is King.[8]

Prayers

Lord Jesus Christ, in this waiting time, help me to live every day to the full—which may include doing nothing—and yet to live every day as though it were my last, so that whenever you come, I may be ready to greet you with gladness, joy and welcoming love. Amen

Our heavenly Father, as we prepare for Christmas, help us to find time in our busy lives for quiet thought and prayer; that we may reflect on the wonder of your love and allow the story of our Saviour's birth to penetrate our hearts and minds. So may our joy be deeper, our worship more real and our lives worthier of all that you have done for us through the coming of your Son, Jesus Christ our Lord. Amen

Invitations

Christmas and New Year are very often times when we might receive invitations for get-togethers of one sort or another.

This reflection, on the theme of invitations, can be used either for a day's retreat or as three separate reflections of about an hour each.

When the postman drops an envelope through my letter-box that contains an invitation, maybe to a party, a wedding, a dinner or some kind of celebration, I feel excited. Whether I am free to accept it or not, I have a warm sense of being included: my company is wanted. I am invited to come— that is, to move towards those who are inviting me, to leave where I am and come to them.

'Come' is a lovely word, unless, of course, it is used as a harsh command: 'Come here!' or 'Come to me this minute!' Also, 'Come' is inclusive: it is the opposite of 'Go away', which means rejection.

Jesus, who came into our world, who moved toward us and lived alongside us, used the word 'Come' on several occasions. Through these reflections we will look at some of them and allow a response to arise within us.

Part 1: Come to me

In Matthew 11:28–30 we read, 'Come to me, all you who are weary and burdened, and I will give you rest. Take my yoke upon you and learn from me, for I am gentle and humble in heart, and you will find rest for your souls. For my yoke is easy and my burden is light' (NIV).

Who is Jesus speaking to? Obviously, to the crowd of listeners at the time, but he speaks as well to all of us who, from time to time, feel weary, tired and fragile. The causes of that feeling might include too much to do or take care of, stress, illness, grief and loss, anxiety, difficult relationships, a guilty conscience, a lack of forgiveness or simply growing older. Any one of these or a combination can sap our energy and make us feel weary.

Jesus is speaking also to those of us who feel burdened, as if we are carrying a heavy weight. We sometimes say of people, 'They carry everything on their shoulders', meaning that they are bowed down with responsibility or concern. Often, these pressures are expressed in our bodies—for instance, in sleeplessness, neck tension and backache, or in a general lethargy.

We can probably all identify with these feelings from time to time. Contemporary life, with all its opportunities and demands, puts many pressures on us. King David, facing many troubles, wrote, 'O that I had the wings of a dove! I would fly away and be at rest' (Psalm 55:6, NIV). In other words, 'I want to escape.' Is this a familiar sentiment to you?

The invitation from Jesus is different. It is to come to him and find rest in the midst of our situation.

Too often we try to sort ourselves out, although that is fine in certain areas of life. We can help ourselves physically, mentally and emotionally through sleep, exercise, healthy eating and spending time with friends and family and on leisure activities. But to find rest for our souls, that deep place within us, we need to come to Jesus. He wants to refresh us and give us peace in our hearts, a sense of harmony in our inner being because we are in relationship with him.

He then makes us an offer—to exchange our burden for his yoke. Maybe, as he said these words, he could see a farmer ploughing a field with a pair of oxen. The animals would have been linked together with a wooden yoke resting on their shoulders. Paul and I were in South America a few years ago, and there we watched a farmer making a yoke for a particular pair of his oxen. It was custom-made to fit them. Jesus offers us a yoke that is shaped just for us, one that rests comfortably on our shoulders and enables us to walk beside him, ploughing the same furrow.

Jesus' yoke is easy, not because he did not have heavy loads to carry (try carrying the load of saving the world!) but because he had the right attitude of heart and mind. He says, 'Learn from me, for I am gentle and humble in heart.'

There were many expectations and pressures on him. He aroused suspicion and hostility from the scribes, Pharisees and teachers of the law. There were many people who followed him, so that it was hard for him to find peace and quiet away from the crowds. There were constant demands on him for healing and deliverance and for teaching.

What he did, then, was to rise very early in the morning and find a quiet place to pray, maybe by the lake or up in the hills. He kept in step with his Father; he was yoked to him. He said, 'I do nothing on my own but speak just what the Father has taught me' (John 8:28, NIV). Jesus is the one who invites us to be yoked to him, to walk in step with him, to learn from his example and the secret of his rest-centred life. He is the one from whom we can learn to live from the inside out, rather than from the outside in.

It is hard to gain access to royalty or the leaders of this world, but we know that the Son of God and co-creator of the universe makes himself accessible and invites us to come to him. Take time to acknowledge, whether you feel it or not, that Jesus is with you through his Holy Spirit.

Invitations usually carry an RSVP because a response is needed. How will you respond to Jesus' invitation?

If you choose to accept his invitation, come to him as you are and not as you would like to be. Be real. The real God wants to meet the real you. Bring the 'stuff' of your life to him—all that you might be carrying and all that might weary you or concern you. Write it down if that helps, or draw a picture showing the many demands that are on you—the projects you are involved in, the various roles that are yours to play, the joyful and the onerous. Have a sense of spreading them out before Jesus and letting him comment.

Is the balance right? Identify where you may have taken on too much or the areas where you feel anxious or overburdened.

When you are ready, make the exchange. Lay down your burdens and take his yoke on you instead. It may be that you need to let some things go, if you feel that your life is overcrowded, or it may be that a change of attitude is needed, such as letting anxiety be replaced by trust.

In your imagination, walk beside him, yoked to him, ploughing the same furrow in God's field.

A prayer

I give myself to you, Lord.
I give you my hopes,
my fears,
my work,
my love.
Set me free, Lord,
to live in you
as you live in me;
to walk with you
as you walk with me;
for your glory.
Amen

Part 2: Come and see

The second invitation to come that we will use for reflection
is at the beginning of Jesus' three-year ministry, when he was
beginning to gather followers. It is recorded in John's Gospel:

The next day John again was standing with two of his disciples,
and as he watched Jesus walk by, he exclaimed, 'Look, here is the
Lamb of God!' The two disciples heard him say this, and they
followed Jesus. When Jesus turned and saw them following, he said
to them, 'What are you looking for?' They said to him, 'Rabbi'
(which translated means Teacher), 'where are you staying?' He
said to them, 'Come and see.' They came and saw where he was
staying, and they remained with him that day. It was about four
o'clock in the afternoon.

One of the two who heard John speak and followed him was Andrew, Simon Peter's brother. He first found his brother Simon and said him, 'We have found the Messiah' (which is translated Anointed). He brought Simon to Jesus, who looked at him and said, 'You are Simon son of John. You are to be called Cephas' (which is translated Peter). (John 1:35–42)

Jesus was raising a lot of interest in the locality and people were curious to find out more about him. He had asked John the Baptist to baptise him, and John had recognised him as the Lamb of God who had come to take away the sin of the world.

John the Baptist had disciples himself, men who attached themselves to learn from him. Two of them, Andrew and probably John, the writer of the Gospel, were intrigued by Jesus and decided to follow him at a distance to find out where he was going. Characteristically, Jesus turned and spoke to them. That is to say, he met them halfway. He made things easier for them, which is what God does for us. It is he who takes the first step toward us. When we begin to seek him, God comes to meet us far more than halfway.

Then Jesus asked them perhaps the most fundamental question in life: 'What are you looking for?' or 'What do you want?' They answered, 'Teacher, where are you staying?' In other words, 'We don't just want to talk to you on the road and exchange a few words. We would like to come with you to where you are staying. We would like to be where you are and talk in depth with you. We have so much we want to ask you. We want to know more about you.'

Jesus replied, 'Come and see.' He was inviting them not only to have a look at the place where he was lodging, or just to come and have a chat, but to come and discover the things that he alone could open up to them.

We don't know what they discussed together but it was a life-changing encounter for the two disciples—so much so that John makes a point of noting the time. It was about four o'clock in the afternoon. Life became new for him when he met Jesus at four o'clock on a spring afternoon. At the end of their time with Jesus, they were convinced that he was the promised Messiah, the Christ. Andrew ran off to find his brother Simon, later to be named Peter, to tell him about Jesus and to bring Simon to come and see for himself.

As scripture does not give us any information, we can only imagine where Jesus might have been staying, but there is a deeper dimension that we can enter into. Jesus lives in the Father's heart. He invites us to come and see where he lives and to make our home there. But the journey to the Father's heart is also a journey to the cross, where Jesus was crucified so that we might be put right with God. There we find forgiveness, acceptance and unconditional love. His home becomes our home, and the home of our being becomes his home.

An imaginary encounter with Jesus

I suggest that you find a comfortable place to sit, with as few distractions as you can manage. Take some time to quieten down before you begin the meditation.

Your imagination is a gift from God and a pathway of the Spirit. You can ask God to use it so that you may gain fresh insight. Don't judge or analyse any thoughts that come to you, but trust them, and your honesty will lead you into a fresh encounter with Jesus. Don't move on to the next question until you have completely finished considering the one before. Take as much time as you want.

Imagine that Jesus has arranged to meet you at a favourite place of yours where you can be completely alone. It's up to you to choose the place. It could be by a lake, on a hillside, on a beach, in a building, in this country or overseas—anywhere. Let a place come to mind, or invent one.

You set out to make the journey to the place you have chosen.

As you draw nearer to the spot, you realise that Jesus is already there. He is waiting for you. What feelings arise in you as you walk towards him?

As you come close, he is standing before you. He is looking at you. What does the look in his eyes say to you? What is your reaction to his presence?

He speaks your name and tells you how glad he is that you have come, and you respond to him.

He asks what it is about this place that is special to you. What memories does it hold, that caused you to choose it as your meeting place?

He invites you to sit down so that you can talk together. He begins by telling you why he enjoys being with you, and you listen to him.

You tell him what he means to you and the effect he has had on your life.

He responds and then asks whether you have any concern that you want to share with him. What is uppermost in your mind or buried in your heart? It may have been there for a long time.

He gives a considered response to what you have shared, and you listen to what he has to say about it.

Jesus speaks again: 'Do you have a question that you would like to ask me?' You take your time to let one come to mind. You may have more.

Again you listen to his reply.

He then asks you some questions, using your name. You do not reply to them immediately, in case you blurt out a trite, thoughtless answer. Rather, you let them echo and re-echo in your mind, observing how your heart reacts to them, until you can answer truthfully.

He asks, 'Who do you say that I am?'
'What do you want?'
'Do you love me?'

After listening attentively to your replies, he looks you fully in the face and says, 'You have my understanding. I can help you if you will let me. We are together in everything—you in me and I in you; you working with me and I working with you. Though you cannot see me, my Spirit is always with you.'

What does it feel like to hear those words of Jesus?

The time has come for him to go, so together you look ahead. What kind of future do you want your relationship to have? In what ways can you develop your side of it?

Your personal encounter has come to an end. You bring your conversation to a close and say 'goodbye' to each other. You look around at this special place, now made even more special by sharing it with him.

Of course, in real life there is no parting, for Jesus has promised to be with us always by his Spirit. We do not go home alone—ever.

Before ending this exercise you may want to:

- continue in conversation with Jesus. It can be helpful to write down any thoughts that come to you.
- reflect further on the moods you experienced in the encounter—whether they were positive or negative.
- think more about your answers to his questions:
    * Who do you say that I am?
    * What do you want?
    * Do you love me?

Part 3: Don't be afraid—come!

This third meditation is based on the events described in Matthew 14, where we read of a particularly dramatic 'come' moment between Jesus and his friends.

It had been a hard day for Jesus. It had begun with receiving the terrible news that his cousin, John the Baptist, had been beheaded.

Jesus' reaction was to get into a boat and row to a place where he could be alone to grieve and to talk with his Father. But the crowds followed him on foot around the shore of the lake and were waiting for him when he landed. Instead of brushing them aside and pursuing his own agenda, his heart went out to them. He set his own needs on one side and spent time teaching the people and healing those who were sick.

As the day wore on, his disciples urged Jesus to send the crowds away so that they could go off and buy food. Instead, Jesus chose to feed them miraculously by making five loaves and two fish into enough food for at least 5000 people. When they had finished eating, Jesus sent the crowds away. He told the disciples to get into a boat and row to the other side of the lake. At long last, he could walk up into the hills, by himself, to pray.

It grew dark—stormy dark. A strong wind blew, whipping up the waves on the lake, as it does on Galilee, which is surrounded by hills. The disciples in their boat were being buffeted by the wind and the waves. Jesus, realising that they would be distressed, went out to meet them, walking on the water. When they saw him, they were terrified. 'It's a ghost,' they said and cried out in fear.

But Jesus immediately called out to them, 'Take courage! It is I. Don't be afraid.'

'Lord, if it's you,' Peter replied, 'tell me to come to you on the water.'

'Come. Come,' sounded over the wind and the waves. Peter's faith surged up in him. He climbed over the side of the boat. With eyes fixed on Jesus, he began to walk on the water. What an amazing sensation! Then he felt the impact of the wind and the crashing waves and he became afraid. He took his eyes off Jesus, focused on the rough water and began to sink. 'Lord, save me!' he shouted in panic, and immediately Jesus stretched out his hand and caught hold of him. Together they walked to the boat and climbed in.

Jesus turned to Peter and reprimanded him. I can't help feeling, though, that there was a smile in his voice when he said, 'You of little faith, why did you doubt?' (Matthew 14:31).

Why did he doubt? Maybe it was because he had taken his eyes off Jesus. In the letter to the Hebrews we read, 'Let us throw off everything that hinders and the sin that so easily entangles, and let us run with perseverance the race marked out for us. Let us fix our eyes on Jesus, the author and perfecter of our faith' (Hebrews 12:1–2, NIV).

At times, though, life is like that sudden storm on the lake. We can be sailing along happily and then suddenly find ourselves caught in a headwind of trouble, which may or may not be of our own making. Our lives feel turbulent and overwhelming. We are sure that we will sink below the waves and fear can set in—fear that we won't be able to cope; fear of a diagnosis; fear of not being approved of by others; fear that things will fall apart; fear of failure; fear of what the future might hold for us; fear of another's dependence on us. Whatever the fear, it can drag us down and rob us of our God-given freedom.

Fear has one of two effects on most people. It can paralyse us or we can take flight and find a way of escape. Which of the two ways are you most likely to react?

Fear is not given to us by God; we engender it within ourselves. As Paul writes, 'For God has not given us a spirit of fear, but of power and of love and of a sound mind' (2 Timothy 1:7, NKJV).

'Don't be afraid' is a key phrase in scripture. It was said to Mary at the annunciation, and to the disciples on the eve of the crucifixion, after the resurrection and on many other occasions. In fact, the phrase occurs over 100 times in the Bible, as it is a human emotion that we are all subject to, and God understands that.

In our passage from Matthew's Gospel, Jesus links fear to

doubt. He says to Peter as he takes hold of him, 'You of little faith, why did you doubt?' We can ask ourselves the same question. Whom do I trust? Myself, others—or God, who will never let us down? Trusting God may not mean that our problems are taken away. The wind and the waves were still rough when Jesus and Peter climbed into the boat. But with God's help we will find a way through it, until we are in the boat and the winds die down.

'Do not be afraid' is often followed by 'Peace be with you.' The two go hand in hand. I have always liked a translation of Isaiah 26:3 said to be a literal translation from the Hebrew. It reads, 'He/she will be kept in peace, whose imagination ends with God.' When catastrophes hit us or we are awaiting a diagnosis, our imagination can take a trip all over the place, and in an instant we can be imagining the worst. If we let God be the buffer for our imagination, it is contained and we are steadied, just as a set of buffers on a railway line means that a train can go thus far and no further.

God is in the middle of the storm. We need faith to reach out and hold on to him. When something confronts us, maybe a daunting task, we shouldn't look down and in towards ourselves. This is what Peter did. He began to focus on the storm and on his fear; he took his focus off Jesus.

The advice that is given to sailors climbing up to the crow's nest, high on the mast of a sailing ship, is 'Don't look down. Look ahead.' Peter dropped his eyes from Christ, looked down and began to sink—but he only made this mistake because he had had the courage to step out of the boat. He took a risk and learnt a huge lesson that would stand him in good stead when he became one of the leaders of the early Church.

This is a challenge to us to step out of our comfort zone and go out to engage with the world in whatever way is possible for us. We may be called to be involved in issues of mission, evangelism, human rights, the environment, opportunities for caring or other situations that might come our way. The challenge is to get out of the boat and to walk hand in hand with Christ in his world.

Jesus calls us to come. We need to learn to walk with Christ in our troubled, turbulent world. This will take time. Think about a baby learning to walk, first taking one or two tentative steps before dropping to the floor. Gradually as the gap is widened between the baby and a safe pair of hands, the baby's confidence grows until he or she is off and there is no holding him back.

For reflection

'Take courage! It is I. Don't be afraid' (Matthew 14:27, NIV). What makes you feel afraid? In what areas of your life do you feel that you need courage?

Hear Jesus say to you, 'Come.' Bring to him any situations that may feel daunting or too big for you to handle, just as the wind and the waves were for Peter.

Hear him say, 'Take courage, have faith.' Resolve to keep your eyes fixed on Jesus.

At the end of this reflection, hear Jesus issue one more invitation to you, as he did to the men whom he was calling to be his disciples: 'Come, follow me.'

Winter

For this opening meditation, you will need a Bible open at Psalm 147, and some music with a sense of winter about it, perhaps 'Winter' from Vivaldi's *The Four Seasons*.

- Find a quiet place and sit or kneel in a relaxed posture.
- Allow all tension to drain away; slow your breathing until it is deeper. Be aware of your incoming and outgoing breaths. Relax.
- Affirm God's loving presence and commit yourself to him, saying, 'In the name of the Father and of the Son and of the Holy Spirit.'
- Read Psalm 147 slowly and reflectively and think about how it speaks of God's creation and his care.
- Listen to Vivaldi's 'Winter' or other suitable music.
- Open yourself to the thoughts of the psalm, allowing the Holy Spirit to take you where he will.
- Emerge gently from the meditation and give thanks to God for his goodness, love and faithfulness.

I would like to follow this with a reflection on winter in two parts, which may be used together or on separate occasions. I should note at the start that I am writing these seasonal reflections as experienced in the northern hemisphere.

If we had lived hundreds of years ago, the countryside would have been very different. Greater areas would have been forested. There would have been cart tracks instead of roads, and hamlets, villages and small towns with their citizens living by the work of their hands and surviving on the bare necessities of life. Winter would have brought extra hardship with biting winds, frozen earth and long hours of darkness.

Today we are cushioned from the season's extremes by miles of tarmac and warm cars to drive in; electricity, gas and oil for light and heat; entertainment and information at the click of a button in our homes; instant communication; shops full of food and clothing, medicines and labour-saving devices. Although heavy falls of snow can bring us to a standstill, for the most part the modern world has managed to overcome the worst rigours of winter. This is not true, of course, for the wildlife—the birds and the animals. They still have to face the harsh conditions of the season.

I remember meeting someone who had a dread of winter and the depression that she often experienced during this season of the year. She tried to live in denial and would wear bright summer clothes for as long as she could. For her, winter was a time to be endured, and she hadn't a good word to say for it.

I suggested that she might go out and about with her camera and take photos of anything that caught her eye which expressed some of the beauty that can be found in winter. She ended up making a small book of photos, observations, poetry and quotations and gradually she began to 'make friends' with this challenging season.

As she discovered, there is much beauty in winter, if we have eyes to see it. There are also many images of aspects of God, and in this reflection I would like to lead you through some that come to my mind.

Part 1: Winter images of God

- God of surprises in the unpredictable weather of winter—gales, sunshine, frost, snow, rain.

  'For my thoughts are not your thoughts, nor are your ways my ways, says the Lord' *(Isaiah 55:8)*.

- God of comfort in the warmth, light, hot food and drink indoors, while it is cold and dark or stormy outside.

  'Blessed be the God and Father of our Lord Jesus Christ, the Father of mercies and the God of all consolation, who consoles us in all our affliction' *(2 Corinthians 1:3–4)*.

- God of mystery: the one we cannot fully know is like early morning and late evening mists or fog, when we can only partially see what is around us.

  'Oh, the depth of the riches of the wisdom and knowledge of God! How unsearchable his judgments, and his paths beyond tracing out!' *(Romans 11:33, NIV)*.

- God of beauty, as seen in flaming sunsets, sun glinting on snow, patterns in the ice on puddles, and hoarfrost outlining the trees, making them appear like white filigree.

  'One thing I asked of the Lord, that will I seek after: to live in the house of the Lord all the days of my life, to behold the beauty of the Lord, and to inquire in his temple' *(Psalm 27:4)*.

- God of suffering: he, who knew suffering himself, understands the plight of those whose homes are damaged by fallen trees; those who have slipped and injured themselves; those who are cold and birds that have starved to death.

'A man of suffering and acquainted with infirmity' *(Isaiah 53:3)*; 'Jesus wept' *(John 11:35, NIV)*.

- God, the Father of Jesus Christ, for it is in midwinter that we celebrate Christmas. Jesus, the Light of the world, penetrates the darkness of the world and its people.

  'The true light, which enlightens everyone, was coming into the world' *(John 1:9)*.

- God the revealer is shown in the skeletal shapes of bare trees etched against the sky; spiders' webs and leaves outlined by frost.

  'You show me the path of life' *(Psalm 16:11)*.

- The God of stillness, as mirrored in frosty days when there is not a breath of wind and all is at rest.

  'Be still, and know that I am God!' *(Psalm 46:10)*.

- God the provider: for the most part, animals, birds, insects and plants are provided for in winter; though some may die in extreme conditions, nature is wonderfully replenished in the spring.

  'God is able to provide you with every blessing in abundance, so that by always having enough of everything, you may share abundantly in every good work' *(2 Corinthians 9:8)*.

- God the Creator of the universe, seen in the brilliant stars on a frosty January or February night.

'When I look at your heavens, the work of your fingers, the moon and the stars that you have established; what are human beings that you are mindful of them, mortals that you care for them?' *(Psalm 8:3–4)*.

* The God of fun and humour, seen in children at play in the snow and ducks waddling on ice.

  'There is a time for everything… a time to weep and a time to laugh, a time to mourn and a time to dance' *(Ecclesiastes 3:1, 4)*.

* The God of faithfulness: we can be sure that spring and new life will follow the dormancy of winter. As the poet Shelley wrote, 'If Winter comes, can Spring be far behind?'[1]

  'Your faithfulness endures to all generations: you have established the earth, and it stands fast' *(Psalm 119:90)*.

* The God of hope is revealed in the swelling buds on trees, the tips of bulbs pushing their way through the earth, catkins on the hazel trees and the white bells of snowdrops. 'Hope' is the winter name of God.

  'May the God of hope fill you with all joy and peace in believing, so that you may abound in hope by the power of the Holy Spirit' *(Romans 15:13)*.

Paul wrote, 'For since the creation of the world God's invisible qualities—his eternal power and divine nature—have been clearly seen, being understood from what has been made, so that people are without excuse' (Romans 1:20, TNIV). Nature has wonderful ways of reminding us of God, if we have eyes to see and ears to hear.

Part 2: Winters of the spirit

Being human, we all go through times in our lives and in
our faith that feel bleak, sterile, dark or even hostile. Such
experiences can be reflected in the season of winter.

In grief and loss, the bloom of summer and the fruitfulness
of autumn have gone, the trees have lost their leaves and
birds seldom sing. During times of bereavement or loss of
any kind, we can experience feelings of deprivation and
sadness. What was is no more, and for a period we endure a
keen sense of loss.

We may face a time of waiting, when nothing much seems
to move in a situation, or a hoped-for answer is not forth-
coming and our patience is tested. Nature has to let winter
take its course. Winter does not rush towards spring; it needs
to be endured, however hard it is.

The Meaning is in the Waiting is the title of an Advent book.[2] This may be easier to say than to believe when a period of waiting tests us, but it is true that valuable lessons of trust and hope can be practised when we are helpless to move a situation on. It provides a time of preparation for what might lie ahead. We need to learn to hang in there, as nature does, until the daylight hours lengthen, the sun warms the earth and, once again, the God of faithfulness brings about the miracle of spring.

We may have an awareness of our frailty, especially in old age, which we might even refer to as the winter of our life. We wish we could do what we used to be able to do, and we have to learn to live with limitations. It is in winter that we experience cold, icy conditions that cause accidents. Even in modern life, there are more struggles attached to this season, whether they are to do with shopping for food, heating our homes or trying to dodge infections.

Nature faces difficulties, too, as there is less food around, sources of water may be frozen, and frost attacks tender plants.

Facing hostility from any source can drain us of energy and undermine our confidence. At the same time, there is inevitably some soul-searching to be done to determine whether the hostility is warranted or not, and whether the root of the problem lies in us or in the other person.

Nature has its fair share of hostile conditions to face as trees are battered in strong winds, birds and animals are shot for food or game, fields holding livestock are flooded and a thick covering of snow makes it difficult for animals to find grazing.

An emptiness of spirit may affect our prayer life. God seems absent and there is a sense of barrenness in our relationship with him, which can feel perplexing. Instead of light and revelation, we are more aware of darkness and silence; instead of the warmth of God's love, we experience an emotional coldness and indifference; instead of energy and fruitfulness, all seems sterile. These are very common experiences but they can upset us greatly.

Quite often, in the season of winter, the sun hides itself behind grey clouds and snow-laden skies, but it is always there whether we see it or not, and so it is with God. The fields have been ploughed and many remain fallow, but not sterile, waiting for the spring sowing. Like winter, our own season of 'emptiness' will come to pass. We can look on such times as an opportunity for resting, seeing them as positive rather than negative, a chance to grow up and not rely on 'warm fuzzy feelings'. Sometimes God trusts us with a sense of his absence in order to mature our faith.

Lest we think winter is all doom and gloom, struggle and strife, we should remember that there are days that are invigorating and offer us opportunities for enjoyment that are different from those provided by other seasons. The prolonged darkness means we can draw the curtains, warm our rooms and enjoy reading, listening to the radio, watching TV, pursuing a hobby or meeting with friends. Home can offer us a place of shelter and refuge from the cold outside.

On days when the sun shines, a walk can make us feel energised and alive. We can enjoy the contrast of the cold outside and the warmth inside. When snow piles up, it asks to be enjoyed by the young and young at heart, with sledging, snowballs and snowmen as the order of the day.

You may like to choose a life or prayer experience that is particularly challenging for you at the moment and give some time to explore the issues around it. Let these words of Jean Vanier help you in this:

> *Christ has penetrated into the depths of darkness,*
> *loneliness, rejection, agony and fear,*
> *in order to touch the depths of darkness*
> *in each one of us*
> *and call us to belief,*
> *to call us to walk in this world of darkness,*
> *loneliness, rejection, agony and fear—*
> *hoping, trusting in the resurrection.*
> *So do not turn aside from your own pain,*
> *your anguish and brokenness,*
> *your loneliness and emptiness,*
> *by pretending you are strong.*
> *Go within yourself.*
> *Go down the ladder of your own being*
> *until you discover—*
> *like a seed*
> *buried in the broken, ploughed earth*
> *of your own vulnerability—*
> *the presence of Jesus,*
> *the light shining in the darkness.*[3]

Here is an exercise with a larger perspective.

Think about an event or situation in your life that, while it was happening, felt very bleak and difficult, but, on reflection, was an important time of growth. Jot down some of the key words and phrases that describe how you felt at the time. Then write down the losses that you faced in the situation, things that were taken from you or that you had to give up. Lastly, make a note of the insights, resolves and newfound strengths that you gained from the experience. How was Christ present at that time, and did the experience draw you closer to God?

If, on reflection, you become aware of certain aspects that are still painful and remain unhealed, think how they can best be offered to God for healing and further growth. Ask Christ to help you see the past as he sees it and have it healed at his pace and in his way.

Nature's way

I find it fascinating to reflect on some of the ways in which animals, birds, plants, insects and reptiles cope with the challenges that winter presents. God has designed them with care and given them instincts that enable them to survive. Thinking about the winters of the spirit, I feel that we have something to learn from nature in terms of coping strategies.

When it is cold:

- Animals grow thicker coats and birds have winter plumage for protection and warmth. In times of stress, we need to find appropriate ways to care for ourselves. A thicker 'emotional' coat can guard against oversensitivity, which saps our energy and dampens our spirits.
- Squirrels find food in times of plenty and store it to feed off in leaner times. We need to build up our resources in easier times, taking time to pray and to read the Bible and other spiritual books that can nourish us. Psalm 119:11 says, 'I have hidden your word in my heart that I might not sin against you' (NIV). There is a lot to be said for

choosing some verses that mean a lot to you and learning them by heart.

- Hedgehogs, dormice and bats, among others, hibernate in the winter, which means that they curl up and sleep; their body temperature drops to match the surrounding air and their heart rate slows down. In times of stress and difficulty, it could be helpful to slow down, offload some of the activity that we are caught up in, and instead become quieter and take more rest. It may be only for a limited period of time.

- Trees are stripped of their leaves to conserve moisture and to help them withstand winter gales. They are dormant and at rest. In the same way, we can learn not to waste energy fighting the difficulties but to stand our ground, firm in God, and face the storm until it blows itself out.

- Because a greater number of eyes are an advantage in protecting against predators, birds flock together to find food and for self-defence. When times are difficult, it is helpful to have a support system—friends with whom we can share what is going on for us and friends who will listen and stand with us. Best of all, we can talk to God about our difficulties and ask for his help.

Are there any of nature's coping strategies that you could adopt, which would be helpful to you right now?

A time to be born

'When the fullness of time had come, God sent his Son, born of a woman…' (Galatians 4:4).

The day was closing in as the two travellers from Nazareth, bringing with them the few necessities of a poor Eastern household, neared their journey's end. It was necessary for them to come to Bethlehem because Joseph, being a descendant of King David's line, was required to return to Bethlehem, the city of David, to be registered for the great census ordered by Emperor Augustus. The way had been long and wearying, about 70 miles, and at the very least it would have been three days' journey, whatever route had been taken from Galilee. They probably travelled along the eastern banks of the Jordan River, crossing by the fords of Jericho and on past Jerusalem. At last they reached the rich fields that surrounded Bethlehem—the House of Bread, as its name means. They walked along the valley and then climbed the hill on which Bethlehem is built, through olive terraces and vineyards. Their urgent need was to find shelter and rest. Mary was heavily pregnant and nearing the time to give birth.

The little town of Bethlehem was crowded with those who had come from the outlying districts to register their names, and every house was fully occupied. The inn was full and only a cave, where usually the cattle were stabled, was available. There Mary gave birth to her firstborn son, wrapped him in the swaddling cloths that they had brought with them, and laid him in a manger. The animals were temporarily deprived of their straw-filled feeding trough. We are left to wonder who attended her at the birthing, so far away from her home and family.

Outside in the starry night, shepherds were keeping watch over their flock. Jewish tradition, based on the scriptures, declared that the Messiah would be born in Bethlehem, the City of David:

But you, O Bethlehem of Ephrathah, who are one of the little clans of Judah, from you shall come forth for me one who is to rule in Israel, whose origin is from of old, from ancient days… And he shall stand and feed his flock in the strength of the Lord, in the majesty of the name of the Lord his God. And they shall live secure, for now he shall be great to the ends of the earth; and he shall be the one of peace. (Micah 5:2, 4–5)

Jewish tradition also held that the Messiah would be revealed from Migdal Eder, 'the tower of the flock'. The Migdal Eder at Bethlehem was not the watchtower for the ordinary flocks that were pastured on the barren land beyond the town, but it lay close by, on the road to Jerusalem. The pasture there was used only for flocks of sheep that were destined to become temple sacrifices. These flocks stayed out all year round and, because of their manner of life and necessary isolation, their shepherds were unable to practise religious observances. They were therefore declared ritually unclean, the lowest of the lowly.

The significance of this is clear when you think of John the Baptist pointing to Jesus and describing him as the Lamb of God, the one who would sacrifice himself for the sins of the world.

So it was that shepherds were watching over the sheep that were destined for sacrifice, in the area where the Messiah was prophesied to be first revealed. Heaven and earth seemed to unite as, quite suddenly before their dazzled eyes, an angel stood enveloped in the glory of the Lord and spoke to them, announcing the birth of the long-promised Saviour. An invitation was issued to go and see the infant, born in the City of David. Most extraordinarily, they would find him lying in a manger. After the herald angel had spoken, a host of other angels appeared, praising God.

The hymn of praise ended, the light faded from the sky and the shepherds were alone once more. But the angelic message remained with them and they decided to follow the angel's bidding and go to Bethlehem to see the babe. The infant, who was God, was not shown first to fully paid-up members of the religious establishment but to simple shepherds, who could kneel at the cradle and 'look level-eyed into the face of God'.[1] They were the ones who were invited to worship the baby who would be given the title 'Lamb of God', the one who would be a 'full, perfect and sufficient sacrifice for the sins of the whole world', in the words of the old Prayer Book. It was a radical beginning to a radical ministry.

We do not know what passed between the holy family and the shepherds, but, having seen the child, the shepherds spread the news of the birth and the manner in which they had been told about it. All who heard were amazed by what the shepherds told them. They returned to their flocks, glorifying and praising God for all the things that they had heard and seen.

At this time, many Jews wanted more than the law that God had given to the chosen people after the exodus. They looked forward to the Messiah, who would be:

- a prophet—one who would be like Moses and know God face to face.
- a king—who would be like David and would restore the fortunes of Israel.
- a priest in the line of Aaron—who would deliver the people from the guilt of their past sin.

As we read at the beginning of the book of Hebrews:

Long ago God spoke to our ancestors in many and various ways by the prophets, but in these last days he has spoken to us by a Son, whom he appointed heir of all things, through whom he also created the worlds. He is the reflection of God's glory and the exact imprint of God's very being. (Hebrews 1:1–3)

In Jesus of Nazareth their hopes and expectations were fulfilled, but, sadly, few recognised it.

Let us pause to reflect on the mystery of the incarnation:

When the time had come
that God had previously chosen
for the redemption of humankind,
his Son, Jesus Christ,
lodged on our lowly earth.
He, the incomprehensible one,
wanted to be grasped.
He who was before all time
took his beginning in time.
He who was invisible in his being

became visible in our flesh.
The God who was incapable of suffering
was not ashamed to be
a human being capable of suffering.
The God who was immortal
submitted himself to the law of death.[2]

God became one of us. He took on the frailty of human life and assumed human nature. He remained God from God, but he also became entirely human. He slipped into our world quietly and was born in very humble circumstances. God chose to enter our dark world rather than summon us to meet him in the heavenly places. He encounters us where we are, coming in dependency and weakness, coming as a newborn baby.

There is something very special about letting a baby curl his or her fingers around yours. They will cling on; it will be you who lets go first. Mary held out her finger to her baby and a divine hand closed on it. When we hold a newborn baby, we gaze at the tiny face, searching for a likeness to a family member. What must it have felt like for Mary to gaze into the infant face of God?

After the shepherds had left, Mary and Joseph were once more on their own with their baby son. Mary would have been very tired after the birth, but her mind would have been filled with the wonder of what had happened and the words that had been spoken by the shepherds. Luke records that 'Mary treasured all these words and pondered them in her heart' (Luke 2:19). In the days and years that followed, she would have often contemplated the mystery of God becoming man and the part that she had been invited to play in the most celebrated birth in all human history.

For reflection

O little town of Bethlehem,
how still we see thee lie!
Above thy deep and dreamless sleep
the silent stars go by.
Yet in thy dark streets shineth
the everlasting light;
the hopes and fears of all the years
are met in thee tonight.

How silently, how silently,
the wondrous gift is given!
So God imparts to human hearts
the blessings of his heaven.
No ear may hear his coming;
but in this world of sin,
where meek souls will receive him still,
the dear Christ enters in.[3]

The magi came bearing gifts

In the time of King Herod, after Jesus was born in Bethlehem of Judea, wise men from the East came to Jerusalem, asking, 'Where is the child who has been born king of the Jews? For we observed his star at its rising, and have come to pay him homage.' (Matthew 2:1–2)

Who were these mysterious wise men and what was their country of origin?

It is thought that they were from Arabia and that they were Gentiles. The shepherds, on the other hand, were from Bethlehem and were most certainly Jews. So the infant king was worshipped by both Jewish shepherds and Gentile Arabs—a radical beginning to his life on earth and a sign that he had come to save the whole world.

The wise men are also known as magi, from which we get the word 'magic'. By the third century they were being described as kings, possibly because of a verse in Isaiah that reads, 'Nations shall come to your light, and kings to the brightness of your dawn' (60:3). In the 14th century, Armenian tradition named them as Balthazar, King of Arabia, Melchior, King of Persia, and Gaspar, King of India. But this is all a mixture of conjecture and legend, for they were most probably from a select tribe of priests living in Persia, who were well educated and became teachers and instructors for the Persian kings.

These men were highly respected and regarded as men of wisdom and holiness. They interpreted dreams and were skilled in medicine, philosophy, astrology and astronomy, studying the stars and planets with great diligence. In those days it was believed that the heavens and the earth were interconnected. When something momentous happened on earth, the expectation was that it would be reflected in the heavens, so, if there was a change in the stars or planets, it would signify a remarkable event on earth.

Many suggestions have been made as to the identity of the brilliant star that the magi saw, which led them to look for a newborn king. Around the time of Jesus' birth, there was a conjunction of Jupiter and Saturn, which, because the two planets appeared to meet, made them look like a single unusually bright star. However, it may be that the star of Bethlehem cannot be explained naturally by science, but that it was a temporary and supernatural light. After all, the first Christmas was a time of miracles.

How many magi visited the infant Jesus?

In one ancient catacomb, or burial chamber, drawings of the magi depicted only two, while a third-century catacomb fresco shows four. A sixth-century mosaic in Ravenna has three, and some medieval Eastern lists show a caravan of twelve, with all of them named. Since Matthew 2:11 mentions that three gifts were given to the infant Jesus, it has been assumed that there were three magi, but the biblical text does not number them.

However many there were, they came seemingly out of nowhere, looking for the one who was born king of the Jews. They appear only once in scripture, in Matthew's Gospel, and then disappear as suddenly as they have arrived. These

Gentiles had been drawn to look for a king, not through any knowledge of prophecy but as the result of a natural event in the sky. They travelled many miles not only to find a baby king but also to worship him and to pay homage to the Jewish child.

They travelled to Jerusalem, the logical place for a baby king to be born. At the palace they enquired as to the whereabouts of this special child. When Herod heard about it, he was frightened, deeply suspicious and threatened by the prospect of being deposed from his throne. The magi must have created a stir in the streets of the city, and word would have been passed round about the nature of their quest, for we read that all Jerusalem, like King Herod, was troubled and fearful (Matthew 2:3).

The chief priests and the scribes were summoned by Herod and commissioned to make a search in the scriptures to find out where the Messiah was destined to be born. They quoted a text from the prophet Micah (5:2), which identified Bethlehem, the city of David, as the new king's birthplace. The magi were dispatched to find the child and to bring word back to Herod so that he, allegedly, could also pay homage—a cover story for his real intention, which was to murder his potential rival.

The magi travelled south-west, some 15 miles, to Bethlehem. They approached the place where Joseph and Mary now lived, seemingly directly beneath the shining star. It was not only the star that told them they had arrived, but within themselves they felt a huge surge of joy. The Spirit of God was at work in them, confirming the destination.

Now follows a sequence of simple steps towards worship, which can speak to us in our own encounters with God.

- They entered the house. They did not hold back on the threshold, full of doubts and questionings, asking if this could really be the object of their journeying. They went in.
- They saw the child with Mary, his mother. They opened not only their eyes but also their hearts and minds. They focused on Jesus.
- These great men knelt down and humbly paid homage to a little child. They were the first Gentiles to recognise Jesus as king, an indication that Jesus had come for all people everywhere. Simeon was later to confirm the child's identity when, in the temple courtyards, he praised God for allowing him to see Jesus and prophesied that he would be 'a light for revelation to the Gentiles' (Luke 2:32).
- Opening their treasure chests, the magi offered Jesus gifts of gold, frankincense and myrrh, the most valuable possessions that they had with them. These were the sort of things that people in the ancient world thought were appropriate presents for kings, but I wonder whether they realised how fitting and how prophetic their gifts truly were. They brought gold, a gift for a king who came to usher in the kingdom of God; frankincense, a gift for a priest, whose function it is to open the way to God, as Jesus did for all of us; myrrh, a gift for one who is to die, as it was used for embalming the bodies of the dead. Their gifts foretold that Jesus would be the true king, the perfect high priest and the Saviour of all humankind.

Because of their openness to God through worship, the magi were able to receive a message from him warning them not to return to Herod, and obediently they returned to their own country by another way.

In this profoundly moving story, we see that the God we worship is indeed the God of surprises who, as well as inviting lowly, ritually unclean shepherds to the cradle of his Son, can also motivate Gentile astrologers to travel from afar to worship the child and to offer gifts of immense significance. In the words of the 18th-century poet William Cowper, 'God moves in mysterious ways, his wonders to perform'.

For reflection
Consider the example of worship expressed by the magi and ask yourself some questions.

- Do I enter or hang back? Do I allow in other distractions instead of letting myself be drawn to worship?
- Do I open my eyes to Jesus, letting him reveal his Father to me?
- Am I willing to kneel before him in reverence and adoration?
- Do I bring him the gift of myself, the most precious thing I have to offer?

Consider the words of this prayer:

What can we bring to your sufficiency but our poverty?
What can we bring to your beauty but our wretchedness?
What can we bring to your wholeness but our woundedness?

Made poor, wretched and wounded for our sakes,
you welcome us, wherever we are, whatever we bring.[1]

Prayer

Lord Christ, you are here,
by your Spirit;
not as a newborn child,
nor yet as a man
but as the King of glory.

Lord Christ, we are here,
children of God the Father;
frail in our humanity,
yet drawn by your Spirit
to worship you, Lord of all. Amen

A woman came with an alabaster jar

This reflection is based on the anointing of Jesus recorded in Luke 7:36–50. The story of his anointing at Bethany during the last week of his life (Matthew 26:6–13) deals with an incident separate from this one in Luke's Gospel.

It is uncertain where the event happened, but it is thought most likely to have been at a stopping-place on one of Jesus' journeys.

Read the passage slowly and then enter the story in your imagination as if you were the woman who went to the Pharisee's house and anointed the feet of Jesus.

Earlier in the day I had come across Jesus and his disciples, and I'd stopped to listen to him. There were crowds of people round him, listening to what he had to say. I managed to get myself near to the front, but I was more taken by who he was than with what he said. He was a young man, full of energy and life. Goodness seemed to shine out of him. He was magnetic—I couldn't take my eyes off him! I heard him say something about being a friend of sinners. I had never heard anybody claim to be that. And I knew I was a sinner.

Everybody in the town knew that I was a prostitute who sold my body for money. I felt both ashamed and beautiful in his presence—an inner beauty, I mean, not the kind of beauty

I doll myself up with to attract the men. Well, you can't really call that beauty at all, especially when you compare it with his.

He looked straight at me, as if he had always known me, and I found I could hold his gaze. It was extraordinary—our worlds being so far apart. He didn't look at me as other men do, summing me up immediately as an object to be used. No, his look was steady and good, somehow pure, and I liked myself when he looked at me. I felt honoured by him. No man had ever made me feel like that before.

I wished, there and then, that I could follow him everywhere and never leave his side; learn to become the woman that he had made me feel—but it wasn't possible. I had to earn a living.

That evening, I was standing in the street, talking to some of my friends—the night's work had not begun—when I saw him with his men coming towards us. My heart missed a beat. They passed us by, joking and chatting to one another. My friends called out to them to let them know that they were available, if you know what I mean, but the men didn't reply. They stopped at a house further down the street and I recognised it as Simon the Pharisee's home. They waited for an answer to their knock and went in.

I couldn't concentrate on what my friends were saying—just coarse jokes, I think, about Jesus and his men. Some strong emotion was stirring inside me. Jesus was at dinner and just a few yards away from me. Suddenly, I knew what I wanted to do and I left the group.

I ran back to the house where I was lodging. The owners were my employers. I went to my corner of the room I shared with several girls and found the box that held my most precious possession—an alabaster jar of expensive, perfumed ointment, hidden under a pile of clothes. I wrapped it in a cloth, waited till the group had broken up and moved off, and then made my way down the street, my heart thumping.

When I got to the door, I could hear voices inside and sudden bursts of laughter. I felt afraid, and yet the urge inside me to see him and to anoint him with my ointment was stronger than any fear. It was like a strong love that I had never known before, a kind of love that released me.

I dared to push open the door a little and squeeze myself in. I knew that if I had knocked at the door, I would have been thrown out. The people inside would know what I was.

The room was hot and shadowy, with a light that burned in the centre of the table illuminating the food and the faces of the men who reclined around it on cushions. The air was pungent with spices, herbs, lamb stew and freshly baked unleavened bread. Women were pouring the wine and bringing in more plates of food. Jesus, as the honoured guest, was next to his host, Simon. In the shadows, I crept around to where he was and stood by his feet.

Fortunately, nobody else seemed to have noticed me coming in, but Jesus, being opposite the door, had registered it and for a moment he turned to look at me. I don't know if he recognised me, but in his eyes I saw that same direct, engaging look with a hint of a smile, as if he welcomed me— almost expected me.

Then the tears came. Not sobs but an outpouring of thankfulness, shame, love, longing—a strange mixture. I could not hold them back. They streamed down my face. As I bent over to hide them, they fell on his feet, and he let it happen. I could have wiped them away with the cloth that wrapped my jar, but instead I took off my head covering, unpinned my hair so that it fell loose and, kneeling, I wiped away the tears with my hair—my long, dark hair—and I kissed his feet as I did so. It was a moment of such intimacy, such goodness. I unwound the cloth and opened my jar, took some of the sweetly perfumed ointment in my hands and gently massaged his feet. I had never known such a feeling of love, a love so pure and undefiled.

The room fell quiet about me. I heard Simon mutter, 'If this man was a prophet, he would know who and what kind of woman this is who is touching him. He would know that she is a sinner.' A cold shiver ran through me and I wanted to get out of the place as quickly as I could. Despair enveloped me. I tried to stand upright, clutching at my jar, when I felt a hand on my shoulder. It was Jesus trying to reassure me while replying to Simon—some story about men owing money. I didn't really hear the words, I was just aware of the warmth of his hand. But then he was talking about me, and, placing his hand beneath my chin, he lifted my head. 'Do you see this woman, Simon?' He was making me visible. He was acknowledging me and what I had done, honouring me in front of Simon and all the others. More than that, he was comparing my act of love with Simon's lack of courtesy.

But there was more to come. Cupping my face in his hands, he looked straight at me and said slowly, deliberately, so I could take it in, 'Your sins are forgiven. Your faith has saved you. Go in peace.' I felt enveloped in an enormous calm—you might call it peace. I took his hands in my own, lightly kissed them and thanked him, thanked him from the bottom of my heart. I knew that he received it. Then, with all eyes upon me and quietly, with a new dignity, I left the room and shut the door behind me.

I walked slowly up the street, seeing no one. I kept walking, walking till I left the town behind and came to a field, lit by moonlight, and suddenly the full emotional force of what had just happened burst upon me. I ran. I danced. Eventually, I collapsed on the grass, sobbing with joy. I lay there for a long time until the cold night air forced me homewards. Something had changed in me for ever. I felt clean and free to be the woman God had created me to be—the woman that God knew I was, under the rotten layers of distortion and abuse. The past was behind and, whatever challenges faced me, there was a new life to be lived.

For reflection

What particularly touches you about this story, and what mood are you left with at the end of it?

It is so liberating to know that when we come to God, he sees us as we truly are, with all the potential that he created in us. He sees beyond, to the real us— the private 'me' rather than the public 'me'. He receives anything we bring to him and he sends us out in peace.

Desert encounters: Lent

Jesus is a young man of 30. He has spent his years in the small hill town of Nazareth, where he is well known as the son of Joseph, the carpenter. I always feel that he showed great restraint in not heading off earlier to begin his mission, especially in his 20s, a time when we have energy, enthusiasm and great ideas. But he wanted to do his Father's will and be obedient to his direction, so he waited until the time was right to leave home.

He heads for the river Jordan and to the place where his cousin John is baptising. Much to John's astonishment, he asks to be baptised himself and, as he comes up out of the water, he hears the voice of his Father: 'You are my beloved Son; with you I am well pleased' (John 3:22). It is a combination of two Old Testament quotations: Psalm 2:7, which refers to the Messiah ('He said to me, "You are my son; today I have begotten you"'), and Isaiah 42:1, which refers to the suffering servant ('Here is my servant, whom I uphold, my chosen, in whom my soul delights'). His Father's words express affirmation and love before the challenge that lies ahead in the wilderness.

These words are repeated on the mount of transfiguration before Jesus' ultimate battle with death by crucifixion: 'This is my Son, the Beloved; with him I am well pleased. Listen to him!' (Matthew 17:5). God, his Father, affirms him at both points of need.

After his baptism, the crowd around is open and eager to hear Jesus. They have heard John point to him as the

Lamb of God. Surely this would be a good place for Jesus to begin his mission—but no. Perhaps reluctant to pass up the opportunity, he feels compelled by the Spirit to leave the Jordan and walk towards the wilderness. The Spirit knows that before people act, they need time and space to listen. It will be an important lesson at the outset of Jesus' ministry.

It was the same for Moses, who spent years in a foreign land before his great mission to lead the Israelites out of Egypt, and it was the same for Paul, who spent three years in the Arabian desert before embarking on his God-given mission to the Gentiles. God is not in a hurry and he desires to prepare us well before we take on responsibility.

So Jesus makes his journey to the Judean desert, a stretch of wilderness so terrifying that it is called 'The Devastation'. Some of you may have travelled through it on your way to the Dead Sea. It is made up of sand and shingle, with twisted shapes of limestone and undulating hills. There is intense heat by day but it is chilly at night.

For 40 days and 40 nights, Jesus sleeps under the stars, waking morning by morning to the colours of sunrise. It is a dangerous place with wild animals roaming around, including lions in the time of Jesus. There are occasional streams of water but no food to speak of. And there are no distractions—no cars zooming through or planes overhead as there are today. It is a barren place of solitude. The silence seeps into him and his Father's loving words reverberate within him. Their bond is proven indestructible.

Part 1: The wilderness—a place of testing

It is a place of testing rather than of temptation to sin. The big question facing Jesus is 'How am I going to win this world for the Father? I am the Messiah, with supernatural powers, but how am I to win the hearts of the people for God's kingdom?' The way ahead is fraught with difficulties and dangers, and Satan comes to test him not only in the wilderness but throughout his ministry. The Spirit intends that Jesus will emerge from the test with clarity of vision and clear goals, equipped and empowered for the challenges ahead. Satan has other plans.

The testing would most probably have been an inner struggle. For a start, there is no mountain in the wilderness from which all the known kingdoms of the world could be seen. Even so, it would have been a struggle engaging body, mind, heart and soul.

Given the absence of witnesses, Jesus must have shared his experiences with his disciples, letting them know that because he was tempted and tested, really tested, he is able to help all those who experience times of testing.

Two of the temptations are prefaced with the words, 'If you are the Son of God...'. Had not God just said, 'You are my beloved Son'? But isn't this just how Satan works, making us question who we really are? 'Call yourself a Christian? Who do you think you are?' It is vital for Jesus to know who he is, and John's Gospel, in particular, is full of declarations: 'I am the resurrection and the life' (11:25); 'I am the way, and the truth, and the life' (14:6); 'I am the true vine' (15:1); 'I am the light of the world' (8:12); 'The Father and I are one' (10:30).

Jesus is to hear the words 'If you are the Son of God…' three years later, spoken at his trial by the high priest ('Tell us if you are the Messiah, the Son of God', Matthew 26:63) and by the crowd at his crucifixion: 'If you are the Son of God, come down from the cross' (27:40). The chief priests, the teachers of the law and the elders say the same: 'Let God deliver him now, if he wants to; for he said, "I am God's Son"' (v. 43). But so sure was Jesus of who he was that he had no need to defend himself.

We will now look at each temptation in three parts:

- What may lie behind the temptation?
- How did Jesus counter Satan?
- How did it inform his future ministry? What came out of the desert experience that strongly influenced him in the days ahead?

First temptation: to turn stones into bread (Matthew 4:1–4)

The flat, round stones that litter the wilderness remind Jesus of the bread that is baked locally. At the back of this temptation is his gnawing hunger after weeks of fasting. Flat stones into bread—he knows he has the power to do it. Surely there is no harm in this: it is right to look after yourself. But he summons up the strength to resist, knowing that he must not use his supernatural powers to gratify himself.

He counters the temptation with scripture, Deuteronomy 8:3: 'One does not live by bread alone, but by every word that comes from the mouth of the Lord.' The previous verse from Deuteronomy is also applicable to his situation, and

Jesus would have known the context of the words he quoted, words spoken by Moses to the children of Israel after he had spent 40 days and nights alone with God on Mount Sinai: 'Remember the long way that the Lord your God has led you these forty years in the wilderness, in order to humble you, testing you to know what was in your heart, whether or not you would keep his commandments. He humbled you by letting you hunger, then by feeding you with manna... in order to make you understand that one does not live by bread alone, but by every word that comes from the mouth of the Lord' (Deuteronomy 8:2–3).

How did resisting this temptation influence his future ministry? Jesus laid great importance on teaching the people the things of God, nurturing them, feeding them with spiritual bread. He did use his supernatural powers to multiply bread on two occasions—feeding the 4000 and the 5000—not to draw attention to himself, but out of compassion, because there was a real need among the people.

He used the image of bread in his teachings:

Jesus said to them, 'Very truly, I tell you, it was not Moses who gave you the bread from heaven, but it is my Father who gives you the true bread from heaven. For the bread of God is that which comes down from heaven and gives life to the world... I am the bread of life. Whoever comes to me will never be hungry... I have come down from heaven, not to do my own will, but the will of him who sent me.' (John 6:32–33, 35, 38)

Never has bread been given a greater significance than when, at the Passover supper, only hours before he was arrested, Jesus took bread, gave thanks and broke it, and gave it to his friends, saying. 'This is my body given for you.' This awesome act is what we remember every time we participate in the Eucharist.

For reflection

Take time to think about what Jesus meant when he said. 'I am the bread of life.' What does that mean for you?

How do you interpret the line in the prayer that he taught his disciples: 'Give us this day our daily bread'?

Jesus said, 'Whoever comes to me will never be hungry.' What are you hungry for? How can Jesus fill that hunger?

In what ways is our world hungry and in need? How can God use you to feed the hungry?

Prayer

This is a prayer from workers in community soup kitchens in the shanty towns of Lima, Peru.

God, food of the poor;
Christ our bread,
give us a taste of the tender bread
from your creation's table;
bread newly taken
from your heart's oven,
food that comforts and nourishes us.
A fraternal loaf that makes us human
joined hand in hand, working and sharing.
A warm loaf that makes us a family;
sacrament of your body,
your wounded people.[1]

Second temptation: to be spectacular (Matthew 4:5-7)

In his imagination, Jesus sees himself standing on the pinnacle of the temple in Jerusalem, the holy city, with a sheer drop of about 400 feet below him. The devil puts the thought into his mind that if he will throw himself down to the temple courtyard, God will surely send angels to protect him, for it is written in scripture. Satan quotes Psalm 91:11-12: 'He will command his angels concerning you to guard you in all your ways. On their hands they will bear you up, so that you will not dash your foot against a stone.'

This testing is about the manner in which Jesus will go about his mission. Would he create a sensation, make a big impact and win people's admiration and allegiance that way? It would be a short cut to fame. Word would spread quickly and many would come flocking to hear him.

But he counters it with words from Deuteronomy 6:16: 'Do not put the Lord your God to the test.'

The effect the temptation has on his future ministry is that he shuns popularity and sensationalism. After he has preached in the synagogue in his home town of Nazareth, the people are furious and drive him out of the town to throw him over the cliff. He has the opportunity to prove God's divine intervention, but instead he simply slips away through the crowd and disappears.

After some of his miracles of healing, he told the people who had been healed not to tell anyone about it. His fame still grew but he never courted it or used it to his own advantage. After feeding the 5000, when the crowd wanted to make him king by force, Jesus withdrew to a mountain by himself. He permitted the crowds to acknowledge him publicly only when, to fulfil scripture, he rode into Jerusalem on a colt and those around shouted, 'Blessed is the king who comes in the name of the Lord!' (Luke 19:38).

God's way for his Son did not lie in the spectacular, and in his wilderness experience he gave Jesus the opportunity to learn this lesson.

For reflection

How important to you is popularity? Does it ever lead you to compromise your faith?

In an age when the cult of the spectacular and celebrity status have assumed huge importance, how are we, as followers of Christ, asked to live our lives?

When success, productivity and achievement come to count for too much, what attitude are we asked to adopt, especially when we are caught up in any or all of these?

Third temptation: to bow the knee to Satan (Matthew 4:8–11)

The devil shows Jesus all the kingdoms of this world and their splendour: 'All these I will give you, if you will fall down and worship me' (v. 9).

This is a temptation to side with the devil, to work with him—not to make things too difficult for people; not to pitch the demands of living God's way too high; to turn a blind eye to evil and questionable things—so that people will then follow in hordes. Do it Satan's way, not the way of the cross. Acknowledge that Satan is the prince of this world, and then he will stop competing with Jesus and give him all he wants—the world and its people. Simple!

Jesus counters with strong words, again from Deuteronomy: 'Away from me, Satan! For it is written, 'Worship the Lord your God, and serve only him' (Deuteronomy 6:13).

At a later date, he will be tempted again to take a short cut to avoid the cross, this time by his friend and close disciple, Peter. Having faced the same test in his struggle with Satan in the desert, he will recognise where Peter is coming from, and so his reply would be the same 'Get behind me, Satan! You are a stumbling-block to me; for you are setting your mind not on divine things but on human things' (Matthew 16:23). He hears an echo of Satan's temptation in the desert to take the easier way.

In the garden of Gethsemane, the same struggle is going on—to opt out and avoid the cross. 'Father, if you are willing, remove this cup from me' is his plea. It is a real and agonising struggle for him, but finally, after much anguish, he wins through and is able to say, '... yet, not my will but yours be done' (Luke 22:42).

At the end of the 40 days of testing, Jesus is exhausted. The devil leaves him (for a while) and angels come and minister to him. What a welcome relief this must have been! He is weary of the contest; his body is weak from lack of food and, possibly, sleep, and his mind has taken a battering. But his spirit is intact because he has remained true to his Father's will.

For Jesus, the wilderness was a place of choices. Would he live for self, for popularity, for power or possessions, or would he determine to renounce all these and, instead, set himself towards doing the will of God?

Jesus emerges with clarity of vision and a sure knowledge of the manner in which his mission has to be accomplished, and also with great awareness of the value of solitude, out of which his ministry and decisions will flow.

Interestingly, towards the end of his life and after facing tough opposition from the religious leaders, we read in John 10:40–42 that Jesus went back across the Jordan to the place where John had been baptising in the early days, to the place of his own baptism—the place of affirmation from his Father. In that place, many people came to him and many people believed in him. It was from there that he effectively began his last journey to Jericho and on to Jerusalem and Calvary. It would have taken him through the Judean desert, the same area where he spent those crucial 40 days and nights. No doubt, lessons learned from that challenging period would have come to mind as he set his face towards Jerusalem.

For reflection
Here are some words of Jesus or about Jesus. Read them slowly, a few times over.

Jesus said to them, '… The Son can do nothing on his own, but only what he sees the Father doing; for whatever the Father does, the Son does likewise. The Father loves the Son and shows him all that he himself is doing.' (John 5:19–20)

'I have come down from heaven, not to do my own will, but the will of him who sent me.' (John 6:38)

During supper Jesus, knowing that the Father had given all things into his hands, and that he had come from God and was going to God, got up from the table, took off his outer

---

> robe, and tied a towel around himself. Then he poured water
> into a basin and began to wash the disciples' feet and wipe
> them with the towel that was tied around him. (John 13:2–5)
>
> 'My kingdom is not from this world.' (John 18:36)

I can't help wondering if the prayer that he taught his disciples, which we call the Lord's Prayer, was forged in the crucible of the wilderness. Certainly we could describe Jesus' motto as being 'I have come to do your will, Father, on earth as it is in heaven.'

> *Our Father in heaven,*
> *Hallowed be your name.*
> *Your kingdom come,*
> *Your will be done on earth as in heaven.*
> *Give us today our daily bread.*
> *Forgive us our sins*
> *As we forgive those who sin against us.*
> *Lead us not into temptation*
> *But deliver us from evil.*
> *For the kingdom, the power and the glory are yours,*
> *Now and for ever. Amen*

Part 2: The wilderness, a place of solitude

In Luke 5:15–16 we read, 'But now more than ever the word about Jesus spread abroad; many crowds would gather to hear him and to be cured of their diseases. But he would withdraw to deserted places and pray.'

Jesus constantly retreated to lonely places to pray, to immerse himself in his Father's love and to find his Father's perspective before making any crucial decisions. Working with people inevitably drained him and he needed times when he could escape from the incessant pressure.

We read in the Gospels that he chose to withdraw to the lakeside, to the hills, at dawn, at the end of a busy day, after a bereavement, through the night when he had to make the decision about which men to name as his chosen apostles, and finally in the garden of Gethsemane. We are told that Gethsemane was a garden that he would frequent when he was in Jerusalem. I'm sure, too, that there were many times that are not recorded when Jesus simply withdrew.

He recognised that there was no substitute for spending time alone with God to receive direction for his ministry. He had come to do his Father's will, so it was necessary to discern it. By doing it, he was set free from the need to achieve; he was not neurotic about the success of his mission or puffed up by popularity or dragged down by criticism and misrepresentation. He remained centred and focused, and solitude was essential for him in attaining and maintaining this state of being.

If the desert and places of solitude were necessary for Jesus, how much more are they for us? It is vital and it is our responsibility to build them into our busy schedules.

It was not easy for him to take time out in solitude, because his fame had spread around and crowds pressed in on him and around him, all the time. It is not easy for us, either, because we live in such a frenetic world.

Ours is a wordy, noisy world. Words form the floor, the walls and the ceiling of our existence. It's a bit like living in a huge dictionary! Words come to us in the paperwork we have to handle, in books, newspapers, TV and advertising hoardings, and spoken words come in our daily engagement with people.

We are used to instant this and instant that—instant communication by telephone and email. At the press of a button we have light, heat with which to cook, entertainment on our TV and global connections on our computer. Transport gets us from A to B easily and quickly, and B is often a lot further away than we would have dreamt of travelling a few years ago.

There is so much on offer all around us. Even when we are retired, there are many things we can do, clubs we can join, courses we can take, meetings, church activities, places to see and people to visit. They are all good, but sometimes we become overloaded and find ourselves rushing from here to there, hardly able to draw breath. The amount of time we have never varies but there is so much more to cram into it. Just by the sheer amount of interaction and the expectations demanded of us, we can burn low, try to run on empty and feel dried up.

I once walked downhill in a field above Wantage from which there was a wonderful view across the plain of Oxford. The field was pockmarked with rabbit holes and hoof marks. I needed to concentrate on where I was putting my feet so as not to twist my ankle, but I was missing out on the panoramic view unless I stopped every so often to look.

In our daily lives, in a similar way, we have to keep our eyes on the job and negotiate our way through life, but we need times to stop and see the bigger picture, time set aside for God. Jesus took breaks and so made sense of his work, his activity and his teaching.

Richard Rohr, a Franciscan priest, writes:

Jesus moved back and forth between the desert and the city or where the crowds were. In the city he could have felt himself losing perspective, love and centre and he has to go out to the desert, to the hills to see the 'real' again. And when he is alone in the desert, his passionate union with the Father drives him back to the pain of the city.[2]

That was his pattern—back and forth. The desert is not a place to hide but a place from which we go back into whatever we came from, but with an altered perspective.

For reflection

Where is your desert space—a room in your house, an empty church, a retreat house, attending a Quiet Day, a walk in the country or even a seat on a train? As we are temples of the Holy Spirit, we have, as it were, a portable cell where, even momentarily, we can withdraw and focus on God.

I have a friend whose times with God are at the beginning of each day when she takes the dog for a walk. On her walk she has set points where she pauses and prays and listens to God. She is an ordained church leader and her days are full from morning till night, but her ministry, she says, flows out of those times in the early morning.

The value of time spent in solitude is fivefold:

- It is a place to be alone with God—God who loves us, not a God whom we should fear. It is a place where we can find God in a fresh way.
- It is a place where God can have his way and set his agenda, not work to ours—a place in which to relax and know that God is in charge.
- It is a place of simplicity and vulnerability, for it is a place where we face ourselves and allow a change of attitude to come about.
- It is a place of openness and listening to God.
- It is a place where we will feel the pain of the world because we are close to the Father's heart of compassion. Solidarity will be formed in us.

Questions to ponder

What are the particular pressures in your life and on your time?

What is your pattern of taking time out with God?

In relation to this, is there anything you would like to change or anything you would like to explore further? What specific steps would you need to take?

Coming out of the wilderness

We read in Song of Songs 8:5: 'Who is that coming up from the wilderness, leaning upon her beloved?' After a period of prayer and solitude, we can have a sense of reconnection with God, of being in step with him once more as he leads us on to the next stage of life.

Spring

For this opening meditation, you will need a Bible open at Song of Songs chapter 2, and some music with a sense of spring about it, perhaps 'Spring' from Vivaldi's *The Four Seasons*.

- Find a quiet place and sit or kneel in a relaxed posture.
- Allow all tension to drain away; slow your breathing until it is deeper. Be aware of the incoming and outgoing breaths. Relax.
- Affirm God's loving presence and commit yourself to him, saying, 'In the name of the Father and of the Son and of the Holy Spirit.'
- Read the second chapter of Song of Songs, slowly and reflectively. It speaks of God's desire for a relationship with us.
- Listen to Vivaldi's 'Spring' or other suitable music.
- Open yourself to the thoughts of the chapter, allowing the Holy Spirit to take you where he will.
- Emerge gently from the meditation and give thanks to God for his goodness and love.

After the challenging weather of winter, the earth begins to wake up and green shoots push through the soil; the hours of daylight lengthen and, because of the tilt of the earth's axis toward the sun, the air and ground temperatures rise. Buds swell and leaves uncurl; birds sing and busy themselves with nesting; newborn lambs appear in the fields and suddenly there are daffodils everywhere. The increasing warmth causes new plant growth to 'spring forth', giving the season its name.

Spring is the transitional season between winter and summer and is said to start in March and end in May, but, as Robert Frost writes in his poem 'Two tramps in mud time', the weather is still unpredictable.

> *The sun was warm but the wind was chill.*
> *You know how it is with an April day*
> *When the sun is out and the wind is still,*
> *You're one month on in the middle of May.*
> *But if you dare so much as to speak,*
> *A cloud comes over the sunlit arch,*
> *A wind comes off a frozen peak,*
> *And you're two months back in the middle of March.*[1]

The upsurge and beauty of spring have inspired writers, artists, composers and poets. The opening lines of two poems illustrate this: 'Nothing is so beautiful as Spring' wrote Gerard Manley Hopkins in his poem 'Spring', and 'O to be in England, now that April's here' were the sentiments of Robert Browning in 'Home thoughts from abroad'.

Spring would seem to be the shortest of the four seasons. Before we know it, we are into early summer. The acid lime of the new leaves has turned to green; woodland flowers, that seized the opportunity to bloom because of increased light through the tree canopy, are now over and the freshness of spring has given way to the fullness of summer. I tell myself to get out and about and look at the beauty of spring.

A.E. Housman, in his poem 'Loveliest of trees', is captivated by the beauty of wild cherry trees festooned with white blossom, which only lasts for a short time. He admits to being 20 years old and says that if his life span should be 70 years, then he has only 50 more years in which to see the beauty of spring. He ends his poem with this verse:

> *And since to look at things in bloom*
> *Fifty springs are little room,*
> *About the woodlands I will go*
> *To see the cherry hung with snow.*[2]

How I wish I had 50 springs left to see the miracle that faithfully unfolds at this time of year as God renews the face of his earth!

There are several analogies in the season of spring that could form the basis for reflection. I have chosen two, which you may like to look at together or use on separate occasions.

- Awakening
- New beginnings

Part 1: Awakening

My lover spoke and said to me, 'Arise, my darling, my beautiful one, and come with me. See! The winter is past; the rains are over and gone. Flowers appear on the earth; the season of singing has come, the cooing of doves is heard in our land. The fig tree forms its early fruit; the blossoming vines spread their fragrance. Arise, come, my darling; my beautiful one, come with me.' (Song of Songs 2:10–13, NIV)

The Song of Songs belongs to the biblical Wisdom literature and speaks of love in the context of an amorous relationship. I also like to interpret it as God's interaction with me. In this beautiful passage, the loved one is invited to look and see that winter is over, to wake up and to open her eyes to the season of spring, to get up and follow her beloved.

It is so easy to get into a rut—a set way of thinking and of seeing situations and people—that we miss what God is doing, the changes that are happening around us and the possibilities that could open up.

Take a short walk around your local neighbourhood in response to God's invitation to 'arise and come with me'. As you walk, be particularly attentive to your environment and notice the familiar sights and places in fresh ways. Look for signs of new growth and the coming of spring. Let your senses be awakened to this season of renewal and turn your thoughts into praise to the Creator. Pray for the people you see and the houses you pass and for all the life represented in the places where you walk.

You might like to write a psalm, a poem or a piece of prose in praise of God the Creator, or one that expresses your thoughts about spring.

Prayer

O Lord,
You sing in this season of the year—
a song that reawakens our spirits;

You paint the world with beauty
that delights our seeing;

You send fresh breezes
to stir the young leaves;

You drench the land with rain
to soften the earth;

You shine with the sun,
that plants may grow;

Lord of springtime,
We would join with nature
in proclaiming your praise,
O Creator of all that is good.

Part 2: New beginnings

Winter gives way to spring and the creative powers of new life are at work in the rising sap, the fledglings in the nest and the unfurling of tight buds. It is a fresh start and a time of new beginnings.

In the course of our lives, we have many opportunities for new beginnings. There are transitions from what was to what will be. It begins at birth, as we are thrust out from the warmth and safety of our mother's womb to begin life as a separate little individual with our own unique identity. Our first faltering steps start us on our journey through life. Then there is the big leap from spending our time at home to beginning the long adventure of learning, as we start school and perhaps continue to university or college, enrol on a training course, take up an apprenticeship or find a job.

Other new beginnings can stem from moving house,

maybe into a new geographical area, from changing our job or even our career, or committing to a long-term relationship in marriage. The whole cycle then begins again as a new generation is given birth and we have to adjust to a host of new beginnings. But it doesn't end there, for before long we may enter the grandparent stage with all its delights and concerns.

An important new beginning for me was in the area of faith. I was a student when I woke up to the fact that Christianity was not just a creed and a doctrine but that it offered me the possibility of relationship with the living God through Jesus the Son, in the power of the Holy Spirit. This so excited me that I made a commitment that has lasted all my life and has grown in depth and conviction. It certainly gave me a new beginning, a fresh start, and opened me up to the possibilities of service and a sense of community in the churches to which I have belonged. For me, there was a date to my new beginning, but, for many others, their experience is a gradual series of steps that lead to faith.

At some point, we will stand on the threshold of the greatest new beginning of all as we are beckoned to move through death into eternal life beyond the grave. The contrast will be even greater than that between winter and spring. We will stand in the presence of the one who says, 'I am making everything new!' (Revelation 21:5, NIV).

You might like to reflect on the chain of fresh starts that have been part of your life. Just as each winter gives way to spring, so you may be able to trace times when one pattern of life gave way to another.

Do you have a sense of a new beginning in any area of

your life now? It could be in a project that you have become involved in, a new friendship that is developing, a new skill that is being learnt, a move or a change of direction.

Life is like a hanging mobile, moving in the breeze. It is ever changing, making new patterns, never static. We constantly have to adjust to new challenges and differing situations. Just as the leaves and shoots of new growth are tender, so we, at times of change, can feel vulnerable and unsure, but God is faithful and what he has begun in us he will complete, if we allow him to do so.

Prayer

God of springtime,
Give us courage to let go of old patterns,
worn-out beliefs and jaded ways of seeing
when you beckon us to embrace the new.

Parting gifts

This meditation is based largely on John's Gospel, chapters 13—17.

Have you, like me, ever wondered what you would do or what you would say to those close to you, if you knew you only had a very short time to live? I know I would tell everyone that I loved them and I would thank them for what they have meant to me. Would I give suggestions as to which of my possessions should be given to whom? Would I want to pass on some advice or would I need to ask for forgiveness? How would I use the time left to me which would enable me to say 'Goodbye'?

When Jesus realised that the mood around him in Jerusalem was threatening and potentially violent, he knew that the time was fast approaching when he would be put to death. When it came to how to spend his final evening with his disciples, he chose to meet together with them, Judas included, in a borrowed upstairs room of a house where they could share the Passover supper. The disciples would also have got wind of the prevailing mood and were, quite naturally, anxious, afraid and bewildered. What was going to happen to Jesus? Would they be implicated too? How would they carry on without him?

Jesus used their time together to share all that was deepest in his heart and all that he most wanted to say, knowing that soon he would be with them no longer. He was, however, aware that in their anxious frame of mind, there was only so much that they would be able to take in: 'I still have many things to say to you, but you cannot bear them now' (John 16:12). So he chose what, to him, were the most important things to communicate and, in so doing, he left them and us with some very precious parting gifts.

1: The Eucharist or Holy Communion or Lord's Supper

At the Passover supper, Jesus instituted this sacrament. A sacrament is something, often quite ordinary, which has acquired a meaning far beyond itself for the one who has eyes to see and a heart to understand.

I imagine that, in our drawers and cupboards at home, each of us has objects that others might classify as junk, yet we will not throw them out because, to us, they have a special significance. When clearing my mother's house after her death, it was interesting to see what her grandchildren chose to keep—a tiddlywink pot that was used in games with her and biscuit tins that used to hold the cookies that she baked. These items brought back special memories and reminded them of their relationship with her.

Jesus took the ancient symbols of the Passover and gave them new meaning. He took ordinary unleavened bread and ordinary wine and invested them with a deep meaning and significance for all time. As Matthew tells us, 'While they were eating, Jesus took a loaf of bread, and after blessing it he broke it, gave it to the disciples, and said, "Take, eat; this is my body." Then he took a cup, and after giving thanks he gave it to them, saying, "Drink from it, all of you; for this is my blood of the covenant, which is poured out for many for the forgiveness of sins"' (Matthew 26:26–28).

In this way Jesus left us an act of remembrance and a way of being nurtured by him that is so simple and yet so profound. It was not just a matter of words but an action that would involve giving and receiving. Nor is it purely an individual act of worship, but it is for the gathered people of God. It should unite rather than divide us.

This act of remembrance also involves looking forward. Luke writes that Jesus said to his disciples, 'I have eagerly desired to eat this Passover with you before I suffer; for I tell you, I will not eat it until it is fulfilled in the kingdom of God... I will not drink of the fruit of the vine until the kingdom of God comes' (Luke 22:16, 18).

So there is a great feast to come in the kingdom of heaven. What rejoicing and thanksgiving, worship and praise will accompany it!

For reflection
Imagine that Jesus himself is offering you the bread and wine. Read again the words above from Matthew 26. What response do they awaken in you?

A prayer

Loving Father,
we thank you for feeding us
at the supper of your Son.

Sustain us with your Spirit,
that we may serve you here on earth,
until our joy is complete in heaven
and we share the eternal banquet
with Jesus Christ our Lord.[1]

2: An example to follow

Just hours before his arrest, when you might assume that his mind would have been focused on the suffering that lay ahead, Jesus did the most extraordinary thing. He got up from the table and knelt to wash his disciples' feet. Normally, in wealthier circles, servants would have carried out this task—not Jewish male servants, as it was considered too menial a task for them, but women, children or Gentiles. On special occasions, it might be done as a sign of love and respect for a superior—for instance, a wife for her husband or a disciple for his rabbi—but Jesus, who was often radical, reversed the order and, as master, he took the role of a servant and washed his disciples' feet. He did it to let them know the extent of his love and to express the kind of love that they should show to others: when he had finished, he said, 'If I, your Lord and Teacher, have washed your feet, you also ought to wash one another's feet. For I have set you an example, that you also should do as I have done for you' (John 13:14–15). His was a humble, serving love, and he could humble himself willingly because he knew who he was.

Jesus knew that his hour had come to depart from this world and go to the Father... Jesus, knowing that the Father had given all things into his hands, and that he had come from God and was going to God, got up from the table, took off his outer robe, and tied a towel around himself. Then he poured water into a basin and began to wash the disciples' feet and to wipe them with the towel that was tied around him. (John 13:1, 3–5)

And that included the feet of the one who was about to betray him.

If we are to be able to serve others, as he did, surely the clue lies in the fact that Jesus was totally secure in his Father's love. Secure in that knowledge, he had nothing to prove, no desire for prominence or for maintaining his dignity, no need to guard his position or protect his image. He was free to serve.

For reflection

Write down everything you can be sure of in terms of who you are 'in Christ'. Doing this can bring freedom from what might hold you back from serving others.

What opportunities do you have to show care and serving love today?

3: Promises to trust

The disciples were getting scared. All this talk about suffering and about Jesus going away to a place where they would not be able to follow was very disturbing. There was something different in the tone of Jesus' voice tonight. It sounded more imperative.

Jesus sensed their disquiet and spoke to them: 'Do not let your hearts be troubled. Believe in God, believe also in me. In my Father's house there are many dwelling-places. If it were not so, would I have told you that I go to prepare a place for you? And if I go and prepare a place for you, I will come again and will take you to myself, so that where I am, there you may be also' (John 14:1–3).

So this would not be the end of the road. They would see him again. There will be a wonderful reunion not only for the disciples but also for us. Jesus is the trailblazer to his Father's house, and heaven will be where Jesus is.

As Jesus went on talking to his disciples, he made another promise to them: 'I will do whatever you ask in my name, so that the Father may be glorified in the Son. If in my name you ask me for anything, I will do it' (vv. 13–14).

This is a bold promise indeed. However, Jesus did not say that all our prayers would be answered in the way that we want them to be answered, but only those prayers made 'in his name'.

To do something in someone's name means doing it in a way that captures the essence of the other person. It is not enough to tag 'in the name of Jesus' on to the end of a prayer. The prayer itself has to reflect Jesus himself. As the paraphrased version of the Bible, THE MESSAGE, puts it, 'Whatever you request along the lines of who I am and what I am doing, I'll do it.' And why will he answer our prayers? It is so that the Son may bring glory to the Father.

For reflection
Jesus makes other promises in John 13—16. Take some time to read those chapters and discover the promises.

4: A helper

Jesus said, 'I will ask the Father, and he will give you another Advocate (NIV: Counsellor), to be with you for ever. This is the Spirit of truth, whom the world cannot receive, because it neither sees him nor knows him. You know him, because he abides with you, and he will be in you... I have said these things to you while I am still with you. But the Advocate, the Holy Spirit, whom the Father will send in my name, will teach you everything, and remind you of all that I have said to you' (John 14:16–17, 25–26).

'Advocate' means 'one who is called in'. In a court of law, an advocate is called in to be a witness in someone's favour. An advocate is one who is called in to give advice in a difficult situation. An advocate is a supporter of a cause. An advocate can be called in to lift the spirits of those who are feeling depressed and fainthearted—to strengthen them and give them fresh courage.

For reflection
Remind yourself that God has called in the Holy Spirit to be with you always. You do not have to live this life out of your resources alone, for the Spirit is available to guide you, support you and lead you into truth. He is the Spirit of Jesus who said, 'I am the way, and the truth, and the life' (John 14:6).

Lord, sensitise our souls to your Holy Spirit, that we may have an awareness of his work within us. Teach us to recognise his presence and his activity in the ordinariness of daily life. May we take note of his gentle nudges and directives, learn to act on them and live our lives in step with our heavenly Helper. Amen

5: His peace

Jesus said, 'Peace I leave with you; my peace I give to you. I do not give to you as the world gives. Do not let your hearts be troubled, and do not let them be afraid' (John 14:27).

When Jesus died, he committed his soul to his Father: 'Into your hands I commit my spirit' (Luke 23:46, NIV). His body was given to Joseph of Arimathea, who buried it in his own rock-hewn tomb; his clothes fell to the soldiers, who threw dice for them; he gave his mother into the care of his beloved disciple, John. But what should he give to his poor disciples, who for three years had left all to follow him? He left them his Holy Spirit and he left them his peace—peace with God and peace in the midst of all that they would have to face in the future.

The New Testament was written in Greek, and there are two Greek words for peace: *eirene*, which is used 99 per cent of the time and always in the words of Jesus, and *hesychia*, which is hardly ever used.

Eirene is the peace that Jesus is talking about in the passage above. It means peace 'in the midst of...'. It is like the still point in the eye of a hurricane: think of Jesus asleep in the boat in the midst of the storm. It is an active form of peace. We can find that peace, that way of coping, when we are rooted in Jesus. It may mean a struggle on our part until we surrender to God's peace. This is how it was for Jesus in Gethsemane. He recoiled from the horror of what lay ahead and was engaged in a battle within himself until he came to the point of saying to his Father, 'Your will, not mine, be done.' Then *eirene* peace came, and he could face his accusers and those who came to arrest him.

Hesychia, on the other hand, is passive. It means an absence of tension, a tranquillity that even a barking dog or the irritation of a fly can disturb. We say 'It's so peaceful' when we mean that there is quiet and an absence of any trouble.

The peace that the world tries to offer is escape, getting away from it all.

The peace that Jesus offers is peace in the midst of sorrow, danger, tension and suffering. It is peace that is independent of outward circumstances. It is dependent on God alone.

It is a peace that is not the tranquillity of unruffled seas, but calm in the storm.

It is a gift from Jesus, which is interpreted to us by his Holy Spirit.

These are some of Jesus' parting gifts to his disciples and to us who believe in him. He ended his time in the upper room with a prayer for himself, for the disciples and for future believers.

Prayer

Lord Jesus, in your love and compassion you did not leave your disciples comfortless. Instead you spread a carpet of promises at their feet—promises that are sure and to be trusted. In your ongoing mercy and love, we are also inheritors of your gifts. May we treasure all that you offer us and live in the experience of your grace. Amen

A time to die

Each year in the weeks leading up to Easter, the focus of church worship turns to the last week of Jesus' life. Another way to approach the events of that week is through the imagination, letting the events unfold in the mind's eye (see 'The Ignatian way', p. 13). We can allow ourselves to become not only onlookers but participants in the drama of Christ's passion. Through such an exercise we can find ourselves far more engaged with all that Jesus endured in order that he might win our salvation and the salvation of the whole world.

Five reflections follow, which could be used on each of the five days in Holy Week, ending on Good Friday. You will need a Bible, notebook and pen beside you.

- Before each exercise, which could take about an hour, allow yourself to come into stillness, free from any other distractions.
- Commit your time to God. Ask for the gift of his Holy Spirit to guide your thoughts and imagination. Trust him.
- Settle into a comfortable position, but not so comfortable that you will be in danger of falling asleep!
- Read the passage slowly, at least twice.
- Look at the suggestions below if you need a framework, or plunge straight in and see where your imagination takes you.

- After each reflection, write down some of the dominant feelings, moods and thoughts that arose in you, and turn them into prayer.

1: The Last Supper

Read John 13:1–15 and Matthew 26:20–30.

See Jesus joining his disciples in the upper room that they have prepared for the Passover meal, their last meal together. You have joined them at Jesus' invitation.

What is the atmosphere like in the room?

Whereabouts are you in the room and what are your feelings?

Allow the foot washing by Jesus to happen and let him include you.

Hear Jesus speak of betrayal and sense the shock among the disciples. What is your reaction to Judas?

After Judas has left, Jesus takes the bread and the wine and speaks of his body given and his blood poured out. The bread and the wine are passed to you and you eat and drink in the presence of Jesus. Is there anything you want to say or do?

After Jesus has spoken passionately but also comfortingly about his leaving you and about sending you a helper—the Holy Spirit—so that you will not be abandoned, you sing a hymn together and then leave the room and walk to the Mount of Olives.

2: The garden of Gethsemane

Read Matthew 26:36–56.

You walk with the disciples, down the hill, through the
streets of Jerusalem, across the Kidron Brook and halfway
up the Mount of Olives until you come to the garden of
Gethsemane, a place frequented by Jesus when he was in
Jerusalem. It is a quiet place, away from the noise of the
Passover crowds.

There is a full moon casting shadows among the olive
trees. You sit on the grass a short distance away from Peter,
James and John and from Jesus.

Although you feel sleepy, you are able to stay awake
enough to hear what Jesus is calling out. You have never seen
him grieved and agitated like this before. What feelings arise
in you?

After his time in prayer, he wakes up his sleeping disciples
with a rebuke.

Hearing sounds in the distance, he realises that it is the
approach of his betrayer with soldiers and an angry crowd
armed with spears and clubs.

Watch the scene as Judas steps forward to kiss Jesus, his friend and master.

Peter raises his sword and strikes the high priest's servant, Malchus, cutting off his ear. There are screams of pain and another rebuke from Jesus before he reaches out his hand to heal Malchus.

The atmosphere is highly charged. Where are you?

In the uproar, you notice the disciples slipping away into the night. You follow the mob leading Jesus, bound by ropes, back to Jerusalem and to the house of Caiaphas, the high priest.

Pause for reflection
What feelings have arisen in you through this meditation?

Imagine Jesus sitting beside you and open your heart to him.

3: The house of Caiaphas

Read Matthew 26:31–35; Luke 22:61–62 and Matthew 26:57–75. You could choose to be an onlooker or you may choose to be Peter.

A door is open and you slip into the courtyard of the high priest's house. Guards are mingling with the crowd that has gathered there. Food and drink are being served. Everyone wants to know what the verdict will be for Jesus. Your attention is drawn to an open window. Through it you can see

Jesus standing before his accusers. You stand close and listen to the conversation that is going on. His life is in their hands.

You catch sight of Peter and move to stand next to him. At the same time, a servant girl brushes past you and appears to recognise Peter. You watch as the drama plays out and three times Peter denies ever knowing Jesus. What are your reactions?

A cock crows at the same time as Jesus is hustled out of the house. He stops and looks at Peter, who weeps in shame.

Pause for reflection
What feelings have arisen in you through this meditation?
Imagine Jesus sitting beside you and open your heart to him.

4: Pilate's headquarters

Read John 18:28—19:16. You could choose to be a guard or an onlooker or even Pilate.

In the early morning, as the people of Jerusalem are beginning to wake up and start another routine day, Jesus, exhausted from lack of sleep and the beatings he has received, is taken to Pilate's headquarters. The religious officials cannot enter so Pilate comes out to them to ask what accusation they bring. They say that Jesus is a criminal and a blasphemer, one who has set himself up as the King of the Jews.

Pilate questions Jesus. Listen to Jesus' replies and note Pilate's reaction when Jesus talks about truth. He is troubled and unnerved. He wants to find a way out of crucifying this man and offers to use his prerogative of releasing a prisoner at Passover. The crowd choose Barabbas instead of Jesus. Pilate orders Jesus to be flogged and the soldiers dress him up as a king in a purple robe and with a crown of thorns. They mock him and hit him.

Jesus is presented to the people. Among them are the chief priests, who whip up the crowd so that the cry goes up: 'Crucify him! Crucify him!' Only days before, when Jesus rode into Jerusalem on a colt, they had shouted, 'Blessed is the king who comes in the name of the Lord.'

Hearing that Jesus claimed to be the Son of God, Pilate is troubled and questions him further. Pilate wants to release Jesus but is disturbed by the Jewish leaders who point out that releasing him will not please the emperor. Pilate cannot afford to fall out with Caesar.

It is the day of Preparation for the Passover. As the lambs for sacrifice are being killed in the temple precincts, Jesus is presented to the people, who, with the chief priests, clamour for his death. Pilate gives in to them and Jesus, the Lamb of God, is sentenced to death by crucifixion.

Pause for reflection
What feelings have arisen in you through this meditation?
Imagine Jesus sitting beside you and open your heart to him.

5: Golgotha, the Place of the Skull

Read Mark 15:21–47. You could choose to be an onlooker, one of the women or the centurion in charge of the execution.

As people get on with their daily business of buying and selling, delivering goods and talking to one another, Jesus is marched along the narrow streets, jostled on every side. Under the weight of the cross beam, he stumbles and falls. Simon of Cyrene is called in to carry the beam for him and the bleeding and bound figure of Jesus is jeered as he follows behind.

Golgotha is reached and the crucifixion is set in motion. Jesus is laid on the ground, offered wine and myrrh, which he does not drink, and then nailed to the cross through his wrists and his feet. The pain is unbearable as he is hoisted up and, with a judder, the cross is dropped into its socket. The struggle with death has begun.

Crucified on either side of him are two bandits. The crowd mock him and deride him; the chief priests and the scribes join in; even those crucified with him taunt him. 'Let the Messiah, the King of Israel, come down from the cross now, so that we may see and believe.'

His mother and John, the beloved disciple, stand near him, as do Mary Magdalene and other women—but where are the rest of his disciples? Three hours have gone by and the sky is darkening.

Another three hours and, although it is daytime, it is very dark. The physical pain is intense but, for Jesus, the greatest pain is the seeming absence of God his Father. He uses what energy he has to call out in a rasping voice, 'My God, my God, why have you forsaken me?' The crowd think that he is calling for Elijah and want to see if Elijah will deliver him from death, which exacerbates Jesus' sense of loneliness and dereliction.

Finally, Jesus gives a loud cry, 'It is finished', and exhales his last breath. As his head slumps forward, the centurion standing opposite him, who has witnessed Jesus' dying over the past six hours and is clearly moved by what he has seen, says with great sincerity, 'Truly this man was God's Son!'

In the temple, there is a ripping sound as the huge curtain that separates the Most Holy Place from the Holy Place is torn in two from top to bottom, signifying that Christ has opened up the way for us to be in the presence of God.

Joseph of Arimathea obtains permission from Pilate to bury the body of Jesus in his own rock-hewn tomb. A very sad group of people process to the garden with the body of the one they love and had thought to be the Messiah. A stone is rolled against the door of the tomb and they return home to grieve.

Pause for reflection
What feelings have arisen in you through this meditation?
    Imagine Jesus sitting beside you and open your heart to him.

For prayer

When I survey the wondrous cross,
On which the Prince of Glory died,
My richest gain I count but loss,
And pour contempt on all my pride.

Forbid it, Lord, that I should boast
save in the death of Christ, my God;
all the vain things that charm me most,
I sacrifice them to his blood.

See, from his head, his hands, his feet,
sorrow and love flow mingled down.
Did e'er such love and sorrow meet,
or thorns compose so rich a crown?

Were the whole realm of nature mine,
That were an offering far too small;
Love so amazing, so divine,
Demands my soul, my life, my all.[1]

Early in the morning

This is an imaginative contemplation based on John 20:1–18.

The crowd breaks up and moves away. Two soldiers remove the nails from the frail, battered form of Jesus and it is lifted down and laid on the ground. We are ready to receive him. Tenderly we wrap his beloved body in a winding sheet and swathe his bloodstained head in a linen cloth. Mary, his mother, is with us and so is John.

A man called Joseph of Arimathea has offered his own tomb for Jesus to be buried in. It is now close to the beginning of the sabbath, so we have to hurry. We want to cleanse and anoint his body with spices in preparation for burial but there is no time. We agree to try and do it after the sabbath is over. We walk with Joseph and the others as they carry Jesus to the garden and we watch as they lay him in the tomb and seal it by rolling a huge round stone across the entrance.

Exhausted, we make our way home. My heart feels as heavy as lead and my mind is filled with ghastly images of the last few hours. It is hard to rest. Sleep will not come. I can't grasp the fact that he cannot have been who he said he was. The Messiah doesn't get crucified. All I know is that I have lost a beloved friend and master, one who had given me a new start and direction in life. It is impossible to think that I will never see him again.

The last two nights and all of yesterday seemed endless. I have relived in my mind the events of Friday so many times, but I have also remembered the times we had together, travelling with Jesus and his disciples. I am heartbroken by the way he has been treated and I long to go and anoint his dear body. I want to show him one last act of kindness.

It's still dark—dawn is just breaking—but I can't lie here any longer. I must go to his tomb. It doesn't even occur to me that there is the stone to roll away. I have prepared the spices for anointing. There's nobody about on the streets and the only sounds are of dogs barking. The moon sheds its silvery light and there are the first streaks of morning in the eastern sky.

The garden is not too far away. I quicken my pace to get there. As I near the tomb where I think he was buried, I feel confused. The stone is rolled back. But it is definitely the right place. I panic, for it must mean that his body has been stolen. How cruel! How unthinkable! I must find Peter and John to tell them. I run back the way I came. How could anyone want to steal Jesus' body?

I come to where the others are staying and knock at the door, shouting, 'They have taken the Lord out of the tomb and I don't know where they have put him.' It takes a while to wake them out of sleep and for my message to sink into their consciousness. But when they hear the urgency in my voice and realise that I mean what I am saying, they are jerked into action and, in a moment, Peter, John and I are running back to the garden.

The sky is lightening when we reach the garden and both men investigate the tomb. It is empty. Strangely, the burial cloths are still lying there, just as if Jesus had vanished through them. Peter and John turn back to tell the others, but I stand rooted to the spot, and again I feel overwhelmed by tears. This loss is too hard to bear. It feels as if my heart is being ripped out of me.

Then disbelief creeps over me: he must be in the tomb. I edge closer to see for myself and find that the tomb is not empty after all. Two figures dressed in white are sitting there, one at the head and one at the foot where the body of Jesus had lain. Who on earth are they? Angels? One speaks to me: 'Woman, why are you crying?' Why am I crying? They can't be angels, otherwise they'd know. 'They have taken away my Lord, and I don't know where they have put him.' I turn away from the tomb.

The sun is just beginning to rise. A man, who must be the gardener, speaks to me. He too asks why I am crying, and who I am looking for. Maybe he knows. Perhaps he is the one who has taken him. 'Sir, if you have carried him away, tell me where you have put him and I will get him.' And then he speaks my name. 'Mary.'

It is his voice! There is no mistaking his voice. I have heard him call my name many times. It's my Lord, my Jesus. He's alive. Death could not keep hold of him. I am filled with joy and fall to my knees. I want to cling to him and never let him go again. He speaks gently: 'Do not hold on to me, Mary. I have not yet returned to my Father. I want you to go instead to my brothers and tell them, "I am returning to my Father and your Father, to my God and your God." With that he is gone from my sight, leaving me to wonder.

I stay a little longer in the garden. I am held in peace. It slowly sinks in that Jesus has risen from the dead, just as he had said he would. We could never understand what he meant, but now I have seen him with my own eyes. I leave my jar of spices where it is. I have no need of it. The sun is warm and the garden is full of birdsong as I make my way back to the disciples' house with the glorious news that Jesus is alive.

For reflection

Jesus lovingly met Mary in her grief. He asked her not to hold on to him. It is as if he was saying, 'Don't cling to me, Mary. I know you want to hold on to this moment and hold on to me, but you need to let go, for the new has come. You need to let go of the past, to move on, to find space in which to grow. Throw off your grave clothes of fear. I am calling you out of your particular tomb. Step out into space. I have given you a gospel to proclaim. Though I return to my Father, I will always be with you through my Holy Spirit. Go and tell my disciples.'

This is what he might have said to Mary as she tried to hold on to the Jesus she had known in his earthly ministry. In what ways might we try to contain him, clinging on to old patterns of belief or behaviour? We can be chained by certitudes, traditions and old ways of knowing Jesus, while he wants to lead us on into a greater understanding, which will be limitless.

Ponder these words from the book of Isaiah:

Do not remember the former things, or consider the things of old. I am about to do a new thing; now it springs forth, do you not perceive it? I will make a way in the wilderness and rivers in the desert… to give drink to my chosen people, the people whom I formed for myself so that they might declare my praise. (Isaiah 43:18–21)

Imagine if Mary had felt too afraid to tell anyone what she had seen and heard in the garden. God took a risk when he entrusted a woman with the precious news of the resurrection and the beginning of new life in Christ. A woman's words counted for nothing in the law courts of Jesus' time. But he also takes a risk when he entrusts you and me with his gospel message. How can we be faithful in rewarding his trust in us?

Prayers

Blessed be God for the faithfulness of Mary,
who went out from the garden
to do her beloved's bidding,
who joyfully proclaimed his resurrection
to those to whom he sent her,
and risked herself in bold believing.

In her proclamation we find courage to speak out.
In her acclamation we gain strength to share our stories.
In her vindication we know the recognition of our redeemed and vindicated lives.

Make us faithful like Mary,
when faith is sent out
into the noon of Easter morning.
Until we come at last
to share in the full glory
of Resurrection Day.[1]

Meeting the risen Jesus

After Jesus' resurrection, he made several appearances—to his disciples, to his friends, surely to his mother (although it is not recorded), to his half-brother James and even to 500 people at one time, as attested by Paul in 1 Corinthians 15:6. In the two following reflections, I want to focus on the two who were walking to Emmaus and on Peter.

Part 1: On the road to Emmaus

This story is told in Luke 24:13–35. It has a wonderful symmetry, as you will see below.

1 Confused about the death of Jesus, the two disciples leave the others.
2 The journey starts in Jerusalem and moves in the direction of Emmaus.
3 The two disciples converse with one another dejectedly.
4 Jesus appears and walks with them.
5 They don't recognise him.

6 Jesus explains to them the gospel message from the scriptures.

5 They recognise him in the breaking of bread.
4 He disappears from their sight.
3 The two disciples converse with one another joyfully.

2 The journey back starts in Emmaus and moves in the direction of Jerusalem.

1 Convinced about the resurrection of Jesus, they return to the other disciples.

Exhausted, disillusioned and bewildered, the two disciples were walking towards the village of Emmaus, about seven miles from Jerusalem. They would not have been the only ones on the road because the Passover celebrations were over and people were returning to their homes. One of the travellers is given the name Cleopas and the other is unnamed. In John 19:25, Cleopas is identified as the husband of one of the Marys who stood near the cross of Jesus, so it is more than likely that she was his companion on the road. It is otherwise suggested, given the vividness of the narrative, that the other disciple could have been Luke, the Gospel writer, himself.

It was a spring afternoon when they walked towards Emmaus, where they planned to stop for the night. As they went, they were deeply engaged in discussion, trying to make sense of all that had happened. They had been disciples of Jesus, not part of the inner circle of twelve but among the many who had been drawn to him and his ministry of teaching and healing.

As they talked together, Jesus came alongside them and walked with them. Instead of revealing himself (which we might be tempted to do when we have a wonderful secret that we can't wait to share), he engaged with them in their conversation and drew them out by asking them what they are discussing. Was he being playful, we might ask? They were so amazed by his question that they came abruptly to a stop and, with a look of incredulity but also with sadness, they suggested that he must be the only visitor to Jerusalem who didn't know what had happened there in the last few days.

Jesus continued to provoke them with his next question: 'What things?' This called for an explanation and they launched into the reason for their confusion.

They had grasped that Jesus was a prophet, who had shown himself to be powerful in his God-centred teaching and actions. They had hoped that he would be the Messiah,. coming to liberate Israel from Roman occupation. But now that Jesus was dead, they realised that it was a lost hope. That was why the two disciples were so depressed, their dreams shattered and their hopes dashed.

They admitted that they were also confused by the reports of the women and some of the disciples who had found the stone rolled away from the tomb, and the tomb empty—but with no sign of Jesus. They really didn't know what to make of it all. Perhaps it was best just to walk away and leave their broken hopes behind.

Now it was the turn of Jesus to rebuke them. He chided them for their slowness to grasp what the prophets had meant. They knew the facts but had not been able to interpret them. Why hadn't they understood that the Messiah would have to suffer before entering his glory? If they had, they would not be so downcast.

As they continued to walk along, he delivered an amazing Bible study, quoting passages from Moses and the prophets and explaining how they related to the Messiah. How sad that we don't have his teaching recorded! It would surely have answered so many questions. As he spoke, their hearts burned within them. The Holy Spirit was at work and they began to recognise the truth of what Jesus was saying and to experience the power of God at work in them.

Almost certainly Jesus would have referred to Isaiah 53 and the predicted sufferings of the Messiah. At this point, it would be good for you to stop and read that passage. In your imagination, hear Jesus speaking it from memory to the two disciples.

The sun was setting as they approached the village of Emmaus. Jesus gave the impression that he would bid them goodbye and move on. He does not force himself upon us but waits for an invitation to come in. That is the precious gift of free will. These two disciples were now so fired up by their conversation with him that they did not want to lose his company. He was no longer a stranger—he had become a friend—and they invited him to stay with them as the day would soon be over.

A meal was prepared and they would probably have re-clined together around a low table. Jesus was the honoured guest but, unexpectedly, he moved from the role of guest to host, taking the bread, blessing it, breaking it and passing it to them. At that moment, their 'eyes were opened', not literally but in terms of understanding. They recognised him as Jesus and they recognised the truth in all that he had said. It was in the intimacy of a meal together, in the breaking of the bread, that they suddenly became aware of who he really was. Could it be that he bore the scars on his hands? Or was it a familiar action that they had witnessed when, as their Rabbi or Master, he blessed and broke the bread at the beginning of meals, or when he fed the 5000?

But at the moment of recognition, he was gone—disappeared. His mission was over and he left them to process all that had happened and all that he had said. They looked at each other in amazement and each of them recalled how their hearts had thrilled within them as he was teaching them on the road. It was all so momentous that they could not keep it to themselves. They had to share the joyful news with the others. Leaving an uneaten meal, they wrapped their outer garments around them and headed back in the darkness to Jerusalem, along the same road that Jesus had walked with them only hours earlier—their road of life-changing discovery.

When they found the Eleven and the other disciples, they were about to give their news when someone else jumped in first: 'The Lord has risen indeed, and he has appeared to Simon (Peter)!' Then the two were able to tell their story, which added confirmation that Jesus had indeed defeated death and was alive.

The two disciples had left Jerusalem as dejected sceptics; they returned as convinced believers. They had left in sorrow; they returned with joy.

For reflection

The two disciples not only believed the words of Jesus, but they also had proof of the resurrection within their hearts. Have you experienced occasions when you knew inwardly that a fresh spiritual insight was true or that a certain course of action was the right one? It is the work of the Holy Spirit to illumine and to guide.

Reflect on how they recognised him through the action of blessing, breaking and sharing bread. Are there ways in which he comes to us through the Communion service, in sharing a meal with others, or in our giving to those who are hungry?

Jesus may walk beside us unrecognised, just as he wasn't recognised by the travellers to Emmaus. He is with us, even though we are unaware that he is present. The risen Christ is not limited, as we are, by geography or time. Often he comes alongside us through others.

Open the scriptures to me, Lord,
show me your face in those I walk with,
put some warmth into my heart.
Encourage me to be hospitable,
to offer my food to the stranger I walk with.[1]

You may like to re-enter the story in your imagination, as one of the two disciples, bringing your own concerns and struggles to Jesus. Listen to his reply.

Part 2: Peter

Peter was wakened from the fitful sleep of grief by the alarmed and insistent voices of women. 'They have taken the Lord out of the tomb, and we do not know where they have laid him.' He eased his cramped body, struggled to take in their words and then, suddenly, his mind was engaged. They must be talking about Jesus. In no time he was up and ready to go with Mary Magdalene to see for himself. John came with them.

They ran through the streets of Jerusalem as people were beginning to go about their daily business, until they reached the garden and the tomb where Jesus' body had been placed. John arrived first, peered into the empty tomb but did not enter. Peter, breathless, arrived on the scene and, without hesitation, entered the tomb. There was enough light to see the linen shroud and head wrap, hardly disturbed, lying there. But the body had gone.

John then entered the tomb. Jesus' prophecy that he would rise again on the third day came flooding back to him and he realised that he was witnessing the resurrection. He was filled with faith as they returned to the rest of the disciples, but Peter was not so sure. How could the stone be rolled away unless the body had been stolen? His mind was in turmoil and he did not know what to believe.

Later that day, some time between the departure of the two disciples for Emmaus and their return, we are told that Jesus appeared to Peter (Luke 24:34), and we get the feeling that Peter was on his own at the time. What a loving act, to seek out the man who had let him down so badly! I wonder what the nature of the conversation was that they had with each other. No doubt Peter would have raised the subject of his denials. He would have remembered with pain and embarrassment how, when asked by various people in the courtyard of Caiaphas' house whether he knew or had been with Jesus, he had vehemently denied ever knowing him. I am sure that Jesus would have known what was in Peter's heart and would have responded with understanding and forgiveness.

Peter would have witnessed the other appearances of Jesus over the next few days, and a week later he and six of the disciples were back in Galilee. Jesus had told them to go there and wait until he came to them and told them what to do.

Peter decided to take the boat out and go night-fishing on the lake, along with his six companions. They fished all night but caught nothing. As dawn broke and the sky lightened, they became aware of a figure standing on the shore. They did not realise that it was Jesus.

The man called them 'friends' and asked if they had caught any fish. 'No' was their reply. Then came the order to throw the net out on the right side of the boat. They obliged and, to their astonishment, they were unable to haul the net in because of the large catch of fish. History was repeating itself, for had not the same happened at the point of Jesus' calling them to follow him?

The moment of recognition came to John and he said to his companions, 'It is the Lord!' But it was Peter who was the man of action. He put on his discarded outer garment, wrapped it tightly around him and jumped into the water. He swam the hundred metres to the beach, followed by the others in the boat, towing the haul of fish. His love, devotion and loyalty to Jesus would have been rekindled as a result of their meeting together and he wanted to do everything he could to prove it.

Jesus was cooking some fish and bread on a charcoal fire that he had lit on the beach. He could have provided all that they needed, but instead he asked them to bring some of the fish they had caught. Again it was Peter who jumped to it, boarded the boat, unhooked the net and dragged it ashore. They counted 153 large fish. Although the catch was great, there were no tears in the net that needed to be mended.

'Come and have breakfast,' Jesus said. He took the bread, broke it and gave it to them, and he did the same with the fish. They did not need to ask who he was because they knew it was their Lord. What an extraordinary barbecued breakfast they shared together at break of day!

Only days before, Peter had been by a fire in the high priest's courtyard and he had denied knowing Jesus; now he was by a fire on the beach with the Lord he had denied. After they had finished eating, Jesus took Peter on one side. Maybe they strolled along the beach, because, at one point, Peter turned round and saw John following them. Although, no doubt, the subject of the denials would have come up in their previous meeting together, Jesus knew how difficult it was for Peter to forgive himself and even to believe that Jesus had really forgiven him.

Jesus knew how important it was for Peter to confront the issue once more, so that he might know that he was truly forgiven. The sign would be that Jesus was prepared to entrust him with a specific pastoral ministry. Just as Peter had denied Jesus three times, so Jesus asked Peter the same question three times: 'Do you love me?' Peter was puzzled and a little upset that Jesus should have to ask the question. 'Lord, you know that I love you,' he replied each time, and in return he received a commission to feed and look after Christ's sheep—the flock of new believers that would be gathered into the infant Church.

But no sooner had Peter been entrusted with his new responsibilities than Jesus looked ahead to the suffering that Peter, as an old man, would experience. One day, Jesus said, 'You will stretch out your hands, and someone else will fasten a belt around you and take you where you do not wish to go.' He was foretelling Peter's death, which tradition holds was by crucifixion in Rome in AD64. He would become a martyr for Christ; there would be no more turning back. So Jesus could confidently reinstate him and issue the same call as he had done three years earlier: 'Follow me' (see John 21:1–19).

The one who had called Peter would empower him through the Holy Spirit and would give him authority to lead the early Church. And so it was that on the day of Pentecost, when the Holy Spirit was poured out on the believers who were gathered together, it was Peter who delivered such a powerful sermon that about 3000 people responded and put their faith in Christ. The Church was born.

Under Peter's leadership, the Church opened up to include Gentiles (see Acts 10). Jesus had said, when describing himself as the good shepherd, 'I have other sheep that do not belong to this fold. I must bring them also, and they will listen to my voice. So there will be one flock, one shepherd' (John 10:16). Speaking to the leaders of the young church in Jerusalem, Peter explained how God had chosen him for a specific task—to preach the gospel message to a Roman centurion, so that he and his household might become believers (Acts 11:1–18). God had confirmed that this was his plan by giving the Holy Spirit to these Gentiles as well as to the Jews, so that there would be no distinction between them. We are all members of his one flock.

We also have two of Peter's letters recorded in the New Testament. I end with some verses from his first letter, which reveal the amazing journey this man had made from weakness to strength, from failure to recommitment, and from doubt to certain hope:

Blessed be the God and Father of our Lord Jesus Christ! By his great mercy he has given us a new birth into a living hope through the resurrection of Jesus Christ from the dead, and into an inheritance that is imperishable, undefiled, and unfading, kept in heaven for you, who are being protected by the power of God through faith for a salvation ready to be revealed in the last time. In this you rejoice, even if now for a little while you have had to suffer various trials, so that the genuineness of your faith— being more precious than gold that, though perishable, is tested by fire—may be found to result in praise and glory and honour when Jesus Christ is revealed. (1 Peter 1:3–7)

For reflection

- Jesus was well aware of Peter's weaknesses but he could see beyond, to the potential that could be released in him. It is the same with us. He knows the ways in which he can use us in his service, even though we may not feel that we have much to offer. He only asks for an open heart and a willingness to join in what he is doing in the world.

- Luke records that during the Passover meal that Jesus shared with his disciples in the upper room, he gave Simon Peter a warning: 'Simon, Simon, Satan has asked to sift you as wheat. But I have prayed for you, Simon, that your faith may not fail. And when you have turned back, strengthen your brothers' (Luke 22:31–32, NIV). He then went on to predict that Peter would deny him three times.

    We, too, are tested but we can know that Jesus is praying for us. He wants us to come through challenging times into a stronger faith and more effective Christian living. As Paul wrote to the Christians in Rome, 'It is Christ Jesus, who died, yes, who was raised, who is at the right hand of God, who indeed intercedes for us' (Romans 8:34). It is a stupendous thought to dwell on!

- We might have been tempted to say to Peter, after his denials, 'I told you so'—but not Jesus. Instead, after the breakfast on the beach, he asks a profound question: 'Do you love me?' To Jesus, love is at the heart of everything—love for God and love for our fellow human beings, which is why, when Peter reassured Jesus that he loved him, Jesus responded by asking him to care for those who were part of his flock. This is a challenge to us, because we can do all the right things, say all the right things and work ourselves into the ground, but if the motive is not love, then, as Paul puts it, we are like 'a noisy gong or a clanging cymbal' (1 Corinthians 13:1). It is worth checking ourselves from time to time, not only to let Jesus ask us 'Do you love me?' but also to ask ourselves if our motives for service arise out of love or from another agenda.

Prayer

O God, you are the light of the minds that know you,
the life of the souls that love you,
and the strength of the wills that serve you:
Help us so to know you that we may truly love you,
and so to love you that we may fully serve you,
whom to serve is perfect freedom,
through Jesus Christ our Lord. Amen[2]

Thomas

Part 1: His calling

It was cold on the mountain. Jesus was alone, spending the night in prayer with his Father. He had a big decision to make and he needed his Father's guidance. He was 30 years old and had already begun his ministry of teaching and healing around the Galilee area. Many people were excited by what they had seen and heard and had become his disciples, following him from place to place, wherever he went.

Now he knew that he needed to choose a small group of men who would learn from him. Twelve would do. It was common Jewish and Greek practice for a teacher to have a small group of close disciples. But whom should he choose? He continued to pray.

As the first light of dawn broke across the sky, Jesus' mind was made up. Wrapping his cloak around him, he made his way down the mountain to his many disciples camped below. They stirred as he came to them and he called them together. In a loud voice he called out the names of those he had chosen to be his apostles (his messengers, his ambassadors): Simon Peter, James and his brother John, Andrew, Philip, Bartholomew, Matthew, Thomas the Twin, James, Thaddaeus, Simon the Zealot and Judas Iscariot.

I wonder how Thomas reacted when he heard his name called out. Did he feel a rush of excitement? What might have flashed through his mind? 'How will my life change and for how long? Jesus is a risky person to be alongside. He stirs up strong feelings in people, often hostile feelings in leaders. What will it mean for me?'

Then he hears Jesus speaking to the group he has chosen: 'I want you to be with me. I have a message to teach you—a message for you to go out and preach. I will use you to heal those who are sick and you will drive out evil spirits in my name. I want you to do what I do. Are you willing for this?'

Thomas' considered response was 'Yes'. There were many questions in his mind, yet beneath the surface lay a deep sense of rightness, of peace, of 'Yes'.

What did Jesus see in these men, that he should especially choose them? They seemed such an ordinary bunch. There was not a wealthy, famous or influential one among them. Yet these were the men who would help to change the world.

What did he see in Thomas? What was the potential in him that Jesus detected? And what is it that he sees in us? He recognises the potential that lies in each of us. Like Thomas, each of us is called to be his friend, his ambassador, his messenger. What an amazing privilege!

He calls us by name. God names us, not with the name that is given to us by our parents but with the name that is known only to him, the name that is unique to us, that describes the very essence of who we are. God knows us intimately; God calls us by name; God calls us to follow him and to learn from him. We need not fear. In Isaiah 43:1 we read, 'Do not fear, for I have redeemed you; I have called you by name.'

Part 2: His commitment

What an amazing three years Thomas had with Jesus and the
other eleven disciples! He learnt so much because Jesus took
time to teach them. He saw things happen that astonished
him, such as five loaves and two fish becoming enough to
feed thousands of people. He watched Jesus calm a storm on
the Sea of Galilee and even saw him walking on the water. He
witnessed lepers and blind and deaf people being completely
healed. He was around when Jesus cast out evil oppressive
spirits and restored people to their right mind.

On one occasion, the disciples were sent out by Jesus in
pairs to preach and to heal. In Jesus' name they witnessed
miracles happening and reported back to him with great joy.

Over the years, Thomas' love for Jesus deepened and his
commitment to Jesus strengthened. In the account of the
raising of Lazarus from the dead (John 11:1–44), we read
how he spoke some bold words to the other disciples.

Lazarus, the brother of Jesus' friends Mary and Martha,

had become very ill. His sisters sent word to Jesus to let him know, but, after Jesus had received the message, he deliberately stayed where he was for two days. He knew that Lazarus would die. He also knew that God's glory would be seen in the miracle that he would perform—the miracle of bringing Lazarus back to life—so he waited.

When, after two days, Jesus told the disciples that it was now time to return to Judea, their immediate reaction was one of fear. They knew that the religious authorities were out to get Jesus, wanting to arrest him on a charge of blasphemy. They remembered that the last time they had been in Judea, stones had been thrown at Jesus. Thomas alone spoke up boldly. He said to the rest of them, 'Let us also go, that we may die with him' (v. 16).

What a commitment, and what a risk he was prepared to take! Thomas was even prepared to die with Jesus. But once the words were out of his mouth, I wonder if he had second thoughts about the action to which he had committed himself and the other disciples. What would they face in Jerusalem? Had he been too hasty? Sometimes it is easy to 'go out on a limb' (think of climbing a tree and crawling out on a branch, which may give way!) and regret it later. But in this case, Thomas' sentiments were Spirit-inspired. Had the disciples not accompanied Jesus to Jerusalem, they would have missed out on one of Jesus' greatest miracles—the raising of Lazarus from the dead—and it must have been a great comfort to Jesus to hear such loyal words from Thomas.

Risk taking is never easy because it takes us out of our comfort zone. Some people, because of their temperament, find it easier to take risks than others. Such courage always takes us into the unknown, where we cannot foresee the outcome. We could risk failure and rejection, but it can also be the path that leads to change and growth in us, and to new possibilities.

For reflection

Think about risks that you have taken in the past. Where did they lead? What did you learn from them?

What are the kinds of risks that you find hardest to take? Why might that be?

Are there any potential risks that you might be facing now?

Turn these thoughts into prayer, asking God for his help to know what you should do.

Part 3: His journey of faith

We get three more glimpses of Thomas, and they are all in John's Gospel. The first takes place on the eve of Jesus' death. He was having supper with his disciples and together they were celebrating the Passover meal. Just a few hours later, Jesus would be arrested and crucified the following day.

Jesus, knowing that the time of his death was near, took the opportunity of sharing with his disciples all that was on his heart. He wanted to warn them, to strengthen them and to encourage them to look to the future.

Here is some of what he said, as recorded in John 14:1–6:

Do not let your hearts be troubled. Believe in God, believe also in me. In my Father's house there are many dwelling-places. If it were not so, would I have told you that I go to prepare a place for you?

And if I go and prepare a place for you, I will come again and will take you to myself, so that where I am, there you may be also. And you know the way to the place where I am going.'

Here, Thomas interjects: 'Lord, we do not know where you are going. How can we know the way?' In his reply, Jesus makes one of his great 'I am' statements: 'I am the way, and the truth, and the life. No one comes to the Father except through me.'

Thomas, the realist, needs to speak out his confusion, his lack of understanding of what Jesus was trying to say. As a result of his honesty, we have the remarkable statement that Jesus made in reply. It is recorded for us so that we might have understanding and our faith might be strengthened.

Jesus would probably have looked Thomas in the eye as he said, 'I am the way, the truth and the life. No one comes to the Father except through me.' It is as if he is saying, 'You don't have to go anywhere, Thomas; my Father's house is here, for I am the way. As you put your faith in me, you will know that you have come home.'

So imagine Thomas' shock and grief when the one he loved and in whom he believed was brutally killed the very next day, and his body buried in a borrowed tomb.

Grief and trauma affect people in different ways. Some become angry and bitter; some withdraw into themselves and shut down; some become restless and agitated; some want to deny the grief and some need to cling to the people around them for comfort. All those reactions were likely to have been present among the group of disciples as they huddled together in a room, with the doors locked for fear of what might happen next.

Thomas was missing from the group. Perhaps he was one whose shock caused him to withdraw. Maybe he felt completely let down, bewildered, his faith in tatters. Therefore, he missed out on the experience of seeing Jesus appear to the disciples, when, on the third day after his burial, he was gloriously raised from death to life (John 20:19–23).

The second glimpse we have of Thomas is when the other disciples finally catch up with him and tell him what has happened. Thomas, now sceptical, says, 'Unless I see the nail marks in his hands and put my finger where the nails were, and put my hand into his side, I will not believe it' (John 20:25, NIV). Remember, this is the man who witnessed the raising of Lazarus from the dead, but now he cannot believe that the same thing has happened to Jesus.

Jesus waited a whole week before appearing to the disciples again. It must have been an agonisingly long wait for Thomas. Once more, they were in a locked room (John 20:26–31). Here we get our third glimpse of Thomas, for this time he was with the disciples. Jesus knew what had gone on in his dear Thomas' mind and so he turned to him and addressed him first. He said to Thomas, 'Put your finger here; see my hands. Reach out your hand and put it into my side. Stop doubting and believe' (NIV).

Thomas' reaction was, 'My Lord and my God!' He saw; he touched; he believed.

Thomas was brave enough to ask the question that millions have asked over the years. Did Jesus really rise physically from the dead? Thomas needed to have proof. For him, seeing Jesus restored his faith. In a flash of understanding, he cried out, 'My Lord and my God!' and I can imagine him falling to his knees.

Jesus then spoke, not only to Thomas but also to each of us. He said, 'Because you have seen me, you have believed; blessed are those who have not seen and yet have believed' (v. 29, NIV). He might have added, 'They know for themselves that I am the way, the truth and the life—eternal life.'

> ### For reflection
> It is right to ask questions, like Thomas did, when we don't understand, and it is perfectly acceptable to doubt when we are not sure. As long as we are open to answers, God can answer our questions and he can do it in a whole variety of ways. He can lead us from doubt to faith, because doubt can be a stepping stone to faith, not an obstacle.
>
> Bring your questions and doubts to Jesus and let his Holy Spirit of truth speak into your hearts. It is helpful to be specific and to write them down, and then to keep bringing them before God in prayer.

A prayer

Risen Christ,
whose absence leaves us paralysed
but whose presence is overwhelming:
breathe on us
with your abundant life;
that where we cannot see
we may have courage to believe,
that we may be raised with you. Amen[1]

Summer

For this opening meditation, you will need a Bible open at Psalm 23 and some restful music, perhaps 'Summer' from Vivaldi's *The Four Seasons*.

- Find a quiet place and sit or kneel in a relaxed posture.
- Allow all tension to drain away; slow your breathing until it is deeper. Be aware of the incoming and outgoing breaths. Relax.
- Affirm God's loving presence and commit yourself to him, saying, 'In the name of the Father and of the Son and of the Holy Spirit.
- Read Psalm 23 slowly and reflectively. It speaks of God's desire to refresh, restore and guide us.
- Listen to Vivaldi's 'Summer' or other suitable music.
- Open yourself to the thoughts of the psalm, allowing the Holy Spirit to take you where he will.
- Emerge gently from the meditation and give thanks to God for his goodness, love and guidance.

The following reflection on summer is in two parts, which can be taken separately or together.

For me, summer begins with the first sighting of swallows, which is really a bit early as they usually arrive in mid–late April, but somehow they have a touch of summer about them. These remarkably agile little birds have flown from their winter home in South Africa, not only back to our shores but to the same area, even to the very same house and garden and to the nest where they took up residence the year before. It is one of nature's wonders that they can navigate across 6000 miles of land, desert and sea to alight in the same familiar spot. All summer long, they wheel across the sky, occasionally resting on roofs and telegraph wires.

While it is winter in South Africa, these summer visitors, along with other birds such as swifts, finches, chiffchaffs, flycatchers and blackcaps, have flown north to enjoy a period of sunshine and warmth in which to breed and raise their young. In Britain we cannot always guarantee them or ourselves the summer weather that is hoped for. Yet, ever optimistically, we arrange barbecues, outdoor concerts, festivals and fetes, and put on a brave face if rain replaces sunshine. We have to make the best of summer, rather regretting what it does not always give us!

Pause for reflection
What images come to mind when you think of summer?
  What do you look forward to?
  What can be challenging?

Part 1: A celebration of generosity

Nothing deters nature in its joyful burst of life into bloom and leaf. The flowers of spring are over. The woodlands, now with a dense canopy of leaves blocking out the light necessary for plants to flower beneath them, are bare save for bracken and a few plants that can stand deep shade. However, there is a riot of flower and colour in parks, meadows and gardens. Grass is rising quickly, as we are very well aware if we have a garden to look after.

In the fields, the crops are growing strongly. There are slashes of bright yellow and the thickly honey-scented air of oilseed rape; ears of wheat and barley stand tall and up-right in contrast to the graceful, weeping heads of oat. The hedgerows foam with white hawthorn, followed by creamy elderflower blossom, and there is a froth of lacy cow parsley on the verges.

Everywhere there is abundance and a fullness of life. God our Creator enjoys being generous and it is very evident in the season of summer, when seeds sown earlier have come into flower.

I have always enjoyed Muriel Stuart's poem 'The seed shop'. In it she imagines picking up a handful of shrivelled, scentless, dry seeds and sees 'meadows and gardens running through my hand'. Her poem ends with this verse:

> *Here in their safe and simple house of death,*
> *Sealed in their shells, a million roses leap;*
> *Here I can blow a garden with my breath,*
> *And in my hand a forest lies asleep.*[1]

Think of a grain of wheat. Each seed has the power to multiply and produce a plant with a considerable number of grains. Nowadays, with selective breeding, it is possible for a stalk to produce up to 200 grains. Each grain, when sown, can produce 200 more grains. That is a celebration of abundance indeed. However, if the grain harvested is kept permanently in a sack, there will be no more yields. It has to be dropped into the ground, where germination can take place.

Amazingly, grains of wheat found in ancient Egyptian tombs grew and produced a crop when sown in soil and exposed to sun and rain. Jesus evoked something of this wonder when he said, 'Unless a grain of wheat falls into the earth and dies, it remains just a single grain; but if it dies, it bears much fruit' (John 12:24). He was, in fact, speaking of his own imminent death—a death that would bear fruit into eternity.

Throughout the life of Jesus, the generosity of God was expressed in a number of ways. The first of his recorded miracles occurred at a wedding feast in Cana of Galilee, where he turned water into wine—not just sufficient for the feast but 180 gallons of the finest vintage (John 2:1–11).

The feeding of the 5000 is another example of generosity (John 6:5–13). The God who loves multiplication created an abundance of food from five loaves and two fishes, out of which not only were more than 5000 people fed and satisfied, but twelve baskets of food were left over.

Jesus spoke of his kingdom as being similar to a mustard seed, which, even though the smallest of all seeds, can grow into a bush so great that the birds of the air can make their nests in its branches (Matthew 13:31–32).

Jesus' resurrection appearance to his disciples at the sea of Galilee, when they had fished all night and caught nothing, was another occasion on which he showed his lavish provision. In obedience to his command to cast the net on the right side of the boat, they were unable to haul it in due to the great quantity of fish caught (John 21:4–6).

But the greatest and most generous gift of all was his act of total, self-giving love on the cross, to win back, at the highest possible price, all of us who have gone astray. Through Jesus, God overwhelms us with his bountiful goodness. He became poor that we might become rich; he emptied himself that we might be filled. Everything he offers us is free! It is at great cost to Jesus, but it is free to us and he longs that we take it, so that we give him the joy of having his gift accepted.

For reflection

How do you respond to the generosity of God?

What attitude might he be challenging or encouraging in you?

Are there some practical ways in which you might be able to reflect his generosity to others?

Prayer

You can use these words from Paul's remarkable prayer found in Ephesians 3:14–21 (NIV):

For this reason I kneel before the Father, from whom his whole family in heaven and on earth derives its name. I pray that out of his glorious riches he may strengthen you with power through his Spirit in your inner being, so that Christ may dwell in your hearts through faith. And I pray that you, being rooted and established in love, may have power, together with all the saints, to grasp how wide and long and high and deep is the love of Christ, and to know this love that surpasses knowledge—that you may be filled to the measure of all the fullness of God.

Now to him who is able to do immeasurably more than all we ask or imagine, according to his power that is at work within us, to him be glory in the church and in Christ Jesus throughout all generations, for ever and ever! Amen.

Part 2: A song to sing

To wake up around 5am on a late spring or early summer morning and open the window, or, better still, to walk outside and listen to the dawn chorus is a magical experience. It begins an hour or so before sunrise and can continue for an hour afterwards. It can be heard from March to July, although it is at its peak in May. It is mainly the male birds that sing, and it is thought that they are giving out two messages: 'Go away' to any rivals as they protect their territories and 'Come here' to any possible mate.

For a few years at Highmoor, my husband and I arranged dawn chorus events. With a group of friends, we would walk across a field in the early morning mist and head down to a wooded valley. In the distance we could usually hear a cock crowing but the woods were silent until a robin, a song thrush or a blackbird began to sing. Then, slowly, others of those families would join in. The smaller birds, such as wrens, chiffchaffs, tits and blackcaps, added their voices a little later. It is thought that the order in which the birds join in could be related to the size of their eyes: those having larger eyes are able to see better in low light and so they are the first to be heard. By about 7am, the birds have begun to feed and the chorus dies away.

How about getting up early one morning, wrapping up warmly, taking a folding chair and a flask with a hot drink, and going outside to sit with eyes closed and listen to the dawn chorus? It will be a moment to remember.

In summer, birds continue to sing throughout the day until, in late summer, they begin to moult. They then receive their new, more thickly feathered coat in readiness for the colder weather ahead. Only after the moulting process is finished do they begin to turn up the volume of their song once more.

Can there be anything more beautiful to hear than a lone blackbird on a summer evening, melodiously singing his heart out? If you listen carefully, you may hear an answering call in the distance.

God could so easily have created birds to sing with the same vocal sound, but, as in all forms of life, he goes in for variety and distinctiveness. So we recognise the mewing of seagulls, the chatter of sparrows, the hooting of owls, the cooing of pigeons and doves, the wild call of the curlew, the repetitive song of the thrush, the rasping sound of the greenfinch, the trill of the chaffinch, the cawing of rooks, the shriek of swifts and, of course—though rarely heard now—the sound of the cuckoo on the wing.

We used to have a chaffinch that visited our garden each year. His stuttering song would sound like 'I... i... i... it's so nice to be here', and I would agree with him. There was a song thrush that called 'Marie, Marie, Marie' all summer long, and I wondered whether he ever found her! This year we have a thrush in our garden that seems to say, 'Bring it in, bring it in!'

God has created each of us with a unique personality, temperament and gifting. We have inherited genes from our parents but we are unique. We are each created with great potential and each has, as it were, a song to sing in life.

John Powell, a Jesuit priest and author, writes:

> *There is an old Christian tradition*
> *that God sends each person into this world*
> *with a special message to deliver,*
> *with a special song to sing for others,*
> *with a special act of love to bestow.*
> *No one else can speak my message,*
> *or sing my song,*
> *or offer my act of love.*
> *These are entrusted only to me.*[2]

We each have a unique place in the kingdom of God. If we don't look for it and try to fulfil it, there will be a gap, because no one else has our set of circumstances, our opportunities, our personality or gifting to fill that place.

Life is short and somewhat limited if we do not discover our joy, our gifting, where our energy comes from or what we can offer—our song to sing. God calls us to respond out of love, though, rather than because we 'ought' to discover the reason for which we were created!

For reflection

You may not find this an easy exercise, but can you think of one or two words that would describe your main calling in life? What have you been particularly gifted to be or to do in God's service? The real God will want to use the real you, so what is it that gives you energy and enjoyment (even though it may be hard work), and affects other people for good?

Here are some examples. After a lot of thought, I came up with the word 'facilitator' for myself, as I love putting programmes, people and environments together. My friend recognised that she is a 'practical help' to people: she has an uncanny way of knowing what help is needed and when. Another friend recognised the gift of encouragement in herself, encouragement that is genuine and not just flattery. We have all benefited from her gift. Yet another friend realised that her main calling was to be an activator for justice, and became involved in initiatives that raised those kinds of issues.

What about you? What is your song to sing?

It is possible to rush around trying to be what we think we should be and doing everything that people might want, all because we are not sure of who we are. What is ours to offer and what can be left for others who have different gifts? I found it very releasing when I discovered my particular calling. I didn't have to be everything else. My life developed a focus, even though, with the passing years, it might have to change due to a reduction in energy and a different context for living.

Eyes to see

Look around: The gift of sight

In Psalm 139:13–14 we read: 'For it was you who formed my inward parts; you knit me together in my mother's womb. I praise you, for I am fearfully and wonderfully made.'

When you look at a very young baby, you may find yourself drawn into wonder by the tiny fingers and perfect little ears. We are beautifully designed.

All our human life is housed in a body. The body is our earthly home. It is God's provision for us. It contains what we are and what we have become through lived experiences—not only our physical bodies but also our inner worlds. We each have a treasury of memories, thoughts, feelings and experiences.

We carry them around in this envelope of skin—not a hard shell but a soft, sensitive skin. The senses of sight, hearing, smell, taste and touch are God's gift to us. They are pathways through which we understand or make sense of the world about us and the people around us, and through which we can become open to God.

Imagine for a moment that you are not able to hear anything. It is a silent world—no music, no bird song, no sound of the sea, no human conversation or laughter, no warning of danger. Everything is silent. Not just for a little while but for always. What would you miss being able to hear?

Although compensations can be made through lip-reading and signing, these abilities would be dependent on sight.

Imagine that you are not able to see anything. It is a dark world—no smiling eyes of the people you love, no flowers and butterflies, flaming sunsets, words on a page or pictures on a screen. What would you miss being able to see?

There would be compensations through reading Braille, but that ability is dependent on touch.

Imagine having no sense of touch. You are numb. There is a complete loss of sensation. I have the memory of seeing a blind man using his fingers to 'read' Princess Diana's face. Without the sense of touch, we would be even more isolated. What would you miss being able to feel?

We would need others to feed us, but if you take away the sense of taste, you would have no pleasure in eating. There would be no taste of raspberries, bread and cheese, chocolate or whatever else you enjoy. What would you miss being able to taste?

At least you could know what was fresh and good to eat and what had gone off and was risky to eat because of the sense of smell.

But imagine if you had no sense of smell. It is an evocative sense, perhaps the most faithful of all the senses in terms of memory. There would be no scent of roses or new-mown grass, no smell of coffee brewing or bacon cooking, no warning of smoke or the gas left on. What would you miss being able to smell?

Take more time to imagine your world without any of your senses. Let them go, one at a time—no hearing, no sight, no sensation of touch, no taste, no sense of smell. Without our senses there would be nothing to inform our inner being and no stimulus for the brain.

Now retrieve them slowly, one at a time. What response are you left with?

I remember staying at a convent a few years ago. From my bedroom window I could look out on to the garden. One beautiful morning in late spring, I watched one of the Sisters walking slowly along the path below. She was in no hurry and, as she walked along, she would stop to look at a bird in a tree above her and listen to its song, or she would bend to look more closely at a primrose, pull a branch of blossom towards her to catch its scent and stop to stroke the convent cat, which had followed her. I felt a delight in watching her, but then I thought, 'How much more her appreciation would mean to me if I had made it all!' I feel sure that God takes delight when we use the senses he has given us to rejoice in his creation.

Go for a short stroll, or walk out into your garden (if you have one) or look out of a window. Look for tiny things that you might otherwise have passed by. See colours, patterns and shapes in nature. Everything in creation can become a sign and means of God's presence if we have eyes to see. Jesus used his eyes to see, and many of his parables sprang from what he saw around him.

If possible, bring back something that caught your eye and led you into wonder.

Prayer

Open my eyes, Lord,
to see signs of your glory—
mirrored in evening sunset,
shining in the brightest star,
unfolding in flower buds,
frosted on fallen leaf,
flying on wings of birds,
curling in the hands of a baby,
smiling in the eyes of those I love.
Open my eyes and my seeing
will behold you.

Look from within:
The eyes of the mind and the heart

The outer senses are matched by inner senses.

Hearing is matched with the inner voice of conscience that we need to listen to. 'Don't do it', 'Just walk away', 'You need to apologise', 'Don't be afraid', 'Risk it' or 'That person needs befriending' may be among the thoughts that come into our minds. It is a way in which the Holy Spirit communicates to us. The psalmist exhorts us, 'O that today you would listen to his voice!' (Psalm 95:7b).

Touch is matched with the realm of feelings. We say, 'It touched me' or 'I feel touched' when something moves us at an emotional level.

Taste is linked to discernment. We speak of something as having 'a bad taste' or we use the phrase 'to have taste' when we consider having good judgment according to a socially accepted standard. In Psalm 34:8 we read, 'O taste and see that the Lord is good.' The psalmist asks us to discern and experience God's goodness.

Smell is associated with intuition. We are not quite sure of what is going on but we have a hunch that all is not as it should be, and we may say, 'I can smell a rat!' or 'It has a bad smell about it' or 'There is something fishy about the situation.'

Sight is matched with insight and understanding, in the sense of 'I see what you mean'. Maybe we can remember struggling with a maths problem at school: when it was explained, we could say, with relief, 'I see', meaning 'At last I understand.' The phrase 'It's a real eye opener' is also linked to the realm of awareness and insight.

Think of some of the phrases that we use:

- 'In my mind's eye' means the way I see it, the picture I have in my mind.
- 'To envisage' is literally to put sight inside or to see a possibility.
- 'To enlighten' is to give understanding and information. It is the Holy Spirit's work to enlighten our darkness in terms of understanding the things of God.
- 'To imagine' is to project a picture, an image, an idea on the screen of my mind. Imagination is a pathway for the Spirit and one that Jesus used frequently in the stories that he told.
- 'To foresee' is to see ahead, to understand what might be the consequence of a particular action.

- 'Hindsight' means understanding gained from past experiences and, maybe, mistakes. Peter and the other disciples had it when they looked back at the crucifixion (and must have wished they had understood earlier).

We need insight to gain understanding and sometimes what we see with our physical eyes is a gateway to understanding. For instance, what we read in the Bible, in books or what we see on the TV can inform and enlighten us. Watching body language; noticing patterns of behaviour; looking at someone's appearance or expression give us clues.

It is one thing to 'see' with your mind, which leads to understanding, but it is another to 'see' with the eyes of your heart, which leads to empathy, compassion and action.

Jesus saw with the eyes of his heart as well as with his mind. He could see clearly to the heart of every matter and he saw in an attitude of love. That truly is to see. When confronted with a funeral procession in Nain, Jesus saw with his physical eyes what was happening; with his mind he understood the implications for the widowed mother of the dead man, but it was through the eyes of his heart that he was filled with compassion and was prompted to take action: 'When the Lord saw her, he had compassion for her and said to her, "Do not weep." Then he came forward and touched the bier, and the bearers stood still. And he said, "Young man, I say to you, rise!" The dead man sat up and began to speak, and Jesus gave him to his mother' (Luke 7:13–15).

When we need to understand a person, a relationship or a situation, we need time. Only when we take time to look carefully around us do we see things that we might not have seen otherwise, so it takes time to gain the insight needed to understand any situation that confronts us. We need time to pray, time to think, time to talk with others or time to be alone.

We need to ponder the situation, to analyse, to reason, to feel, to view from all angles, not just our own. We may need to look back at the past, at what were the circumstances and influences.

We try to get a bigger picture. Looking at a garden is different when you are standing in it than when you are looking at it from a bedroom window, and it would be different again if you looked down on it from a helicopter. The opposite of having a bigger picture is 'not seeing further than your nose'. Sometimes we are too close to a situation to see it properly. We need some space for a bigger perspective. We can ask God for his view.

For reflection

Here are some words from scripture to meditate on.

For it is the God who said, 'Let light shine out of darkness', who has shone in our hearts to give the light of the knowledge of the glory of God in the face of Jesus Christ. (2 Corinthians 4:6)

When he was at table with them, [Jesus] took bread, blessed and broke it, and gave it to them. Then their eyes were opened, and they recognised him; and he vanished from their sight. (Luke 24:30–31)

I pray that the God of our Lord Jesus Christ, the Father of glory, may give you a spirit of wisdom and revelation as you come to know him, so that, with the eyes of your heart enlightened, you may know what is the hope to which he has called you, what are the riches of his glorious inheritance among the saints, and what is the immeasurable greatness of his power for us who believe, according to the working of his great power. (Ephesians 1:17–19)

Identify a current situation in your life, your family, your church or your work where you know you need greater insight. Ask God for the grace of discernment and understanding to 'see' what ought to happen, and what decisions have to be taken.

Look up: The eyes of faith

There is another dimension of 'seeing' which is a gift from God, and that is faith.

We are encouraged to believe in God, who is invisible; to trust in a Saviour whom we have not met in person, and to be inhabited by the Spirit of God. The Christian life is a walk of faith, as Paul wrote to the Corinthians: 'We walk by faith, not by sight' (2 Corinthians 5:7).

Thomas exclaimed, 'My Lord and my God!' after encountering the risen Jesus, and Jesus replied, 'Have you believed because you have seen me? Blessed are those who have not seen and yet have come to believe' (John 20:28–29).

Peter, in his letter, picks up the same theme: 'Although you have not seen him, you love him; and even though you do not see him now, you believe in him and rejoice with an indescribable and glorious joy, for you are receiving the outcome of your faith, the salvation of your souls' (1 Peter 1:8–9).

It is important to realise that it is not we who see and understand, but God who sees and understands and asks us to trust him. 'Whenever you pray, go into your room and shut the door and pray to your Father who is in secret [or unseen]; and your Father who sees in secret will reward you' (Matthew 6:6).

Jesus is the focus for the eyes of faith. As the book of Hebrews tells us, 'Let us run with perseverance the race that is set before us, looking to Jesus the pioneer and perfecter of our faith' (12:1–2).

The scriptures are the means through which the eyes of faith may gaze on the Saviour. There are strong foundations for our faith, but there is also mystery. In this life we can never fully know God. In 1 Corinthians 13:12 (NIV), Paul says that it is as if 'we see but a poor reflection in a mirror' (which would have been made of polished brass in those days), or, as the King James Version puts it, 'through a glass darkly'.

But the day will surely come when we will behold him with unclouded sight. He will no longer be mystery, for we will fully know him. The verse from 1 Corinthians continues, '... but then we will see face to face. Now I know only in part; then I will know fully, even as I have been fully known.'

Until that day, we can live with gratitude for our physical eyes, which see the world about us and the people in it; for the gift of insight and compassion; for God's willingness to reveal himself through his Spirit; for his gift of faith to believe wholeheartedly in Jesus Christ our Redeemer. We can look forward to seeing him face to face and to the wonderful reunions that will take place in heaven.

Closing prayer

For the gift of eyes
*   We give you thanks*

For the gift of insight
*   We give you thanks*

For the gift of empathy
*   We give you thanks*

For the gift of faith
*   We give you thanks*

For the promise of heaven
*   We bless you*

Father, Son and Holy Spirit. Amen

The tree of life

This is an exercise that will give you the opportunity to stop and take stock of your life as it is at present. It is a disciplined exercise and could take you up to four hours to tackle it in depth, so you will need to choose a time when you are not likely to be interrupted. It would be even better to go away for a day's retreat so that you are not surrounded by reminders of jobs to be done or a telephone to be answered.

You will need a large piece of paper (A3), some scrap paper, a pencil and a rubber. You may like to use some coloured crayons or felt pens.

You will be using the analogy of a tree with its roots, trunk and branches as a way of mapping out your life with its present commitments and relationships.

It would be hard to imagine our landscape without trees. They add so much to the beauty around us at every season of the year, whether dressed in lime at springtime, the green of summer, or dazzling autumn colours—or bereft of leaves but showing the tracery of bare branches etched against a winter sky. They offer shade from the heat and protection from the storm and accommodate a whole world of insects, squirrels and birds. For the most part, they outlive us, and when we plant a tree we plant for posterity. I saw some ancient oaks in the grounds of Blenheim Palace, Oxfordshire, which are about 600 years old and yet have life in them. One, which has the name King Harry, is 800 years old and still bears leaf.

I want to start with some facts about trees, to provide background for the exercise that follows.

The trunk of a broad-leaved tree divides at a certain height into a few thick, upward- or outward-growing branches that divide further and further to form the crown, which may be oval or round depending on the species. This shape provides the leaves with the greatest amount of light and air, ensuring the best conditions for the nourishment of the tree.

The tree is anchored in the ground by means of roots, which also serve to supply it with water and mineral nutrients and act as storage for reserve food supplies. The roots take up the same area below ground as the branches do above.

All the elements for growth are provided for the tree: carbon dioxide in the air, radiant energy from the sun, rain water and the dissolved minerals it contains, and the nutrients from the soil in which the tree is planted. The tree obtains nourishment from the soil through the roots and from the air through the leaves, which are spread out as advantageously as possible. Like all flowering plants, trees bear fruit, reproduce and spread naturally by means of seed.

The way the tree grows is influenced by its environment— whether it grows in open ground with space around it or whether it grows in competition with other trees in a forest and has to reach high to find the sunlight.

The exercise

Before you begin, take some time to sit in quietness with God, your Creator and your loving Father. Ask for the help of the Holy Spirit to give you insight and understanding.

Be prepared to draw a tree on your A3 paper. First, take a piece of scrap paper and jot down some answers to these questions, as you think about what kind of tree might represent you and about the conditions it might grow in.

- What species of tree will you choose—a broad, strong oak, a graceful birch, a tall beech or another?
- Is your tree wide and spreading (in which case you might need to turn your A3 paper horizontally) or is it tall and upright (so that you need to turn the paper vertically)?
- What is the season of the year in terms of your life experience?
- What is the prevailing weather in your life at the moment— for example, sunny and calm, stormy and challenging, cold and frosty?
- What would you describe as the soil conditions of your life—fertile, stony, damp or dry?

It does not matter whether you feel you can draw a tree or not, as your picture can be very basic and simple or as artistic as you want it to be. As you start to draw, consider the following:

- It is the roots that anchor and nourish you. Who or what does that for you? Draw the roots and label each one.
- Thinking of the trunk—what are your strengths, and what do you feel your calling is to be or do? (I found it easier to name my trunk after I had thought about the branches and leaves: see the following points.)
- The main branches are the dominant areas of activity in your life. You may find that some of your branches echo your roots. For example, if your family is a strong root in

your life, you will probably have a branch labelled 'family' too, as family business probably uses a fair amount of your time. The same could be said for church.

- The smaller branches are the specific activities relating to the main branch. For example, if church is one of your main branches, smaller branches leading off would be the specific areas you are involved in, which could be youth work, playing a musical instrument in worship and being part of a weekly home group.
- The leaves are the jobs that are necessary for each small branch. To develop the main church branch further, the jobs would be those associated with each activity, so youth work could involve producing the publicity material, booking the hall, meeting with others to plan the programme and any other jobs that might occur to you.

You could also ask yourself:

- Are any branches damaged, dead or broken off and lying on the ground? These can represent commitments, people or jobs that are no longer playing an active part in your life but are still influential.
- Are there any scars of past wounds on your tree?
- Does your tree bear fruit?
- Is it offering shelter, rest or food for others?

This may sound an exhausting exercise to do in such detail but it is well worth it because, at the end, you will have a full picture of what is going on in your life. When you have finished your drawing and labelling, take a break and walk away from it for a short while.

For reflection

When you return, take a look at the finished result and write down any observations that come to you.

- Is there a branch for recreation?
- Which parts demand too much energy and drain you?
- Which areas give you energy and enjoyment, even though they may involve hard work? Which bits are downright unpleasant?
- Are there areas of duty that are getting squeezed because there is not really enough space for them?
- Do the chosen branches of activity reflect the words that you put on the trunk? In other words, are you doing and being what you feel called to do and be— or is there a mismatch?
- How do you feel about your tree?

Then, in your imagination, walk with God in the garden until you come upon your tree. Let him look at it and comment on it. Listen and then write down what you sense he may be saying. As a result of what you hear, are there any changes for you to make?

Be specific and write on the back of your drawing the steps that you will need to take to effect the necessary changes. Make sure that they are manageable and not unrealistic.

When you have finished, spend some time with your heavenly Father, whom Jesus likened to the gardener (John 15:1, NIV), the one who knows you better than you know yourself and loves you with an unconditional, life-giving love. Commit your way to him and let him guide you in the days ahead.

Keep your drawing and refer to it in a few years' time, noting the changes as life moves on.

He restores my soul

You will need the text of Psalm 23 to read and, if possible, a musical setting of the words to listen to—for example, John Rutter's 'The Lord is my Shepherd', Stuart Townend's recording with the same title or the more traditional Crimond version. You may like to play it at the beginning or end of each part of the meditation.

The word 'restore' comes from the Latin *restaurare*, which means 'to rebuild'. It makes me think of a stone wall that, over the passage of time, has become broken down and needs repairing. These days, it is often too expensive to take the time to put the stones of a wall back in place, and few people are prepared to do the necessary work. It is cheaper and simpler to string some electric wire in front of it to keep the animals in the field.

But God is in the business of patiently restoring us when we feel broken. He will take infinite care and work with patience as we allow him.

'Replenish' is a word with a similar meaning. It means 'to make full or complete again' by resupplying what has been used up or what is lacking, as in replenishing a food store. Another word that comes to mind is 'revitalise'—to breathe fresh life into something or someone, to refresh and renew.

The truth is that we come to the God of Life as we are, perhaps needing to be reawakened, built up, replenished, restored, renewed and revitalised. It is his delight to meet us where we are, for he understands us.

I wonder if Jesus took his idea of being the good shepherd from Psalm 23, which he would have known well. He said, 'I am the good shepherd. I know my own...' (John 10:14). So, when we come to Jesus, we come to the one who knows us and loves us.

Before meditating on the psalm, take a moment of quiet to acknowledge God's presence with you and to become aware of your own need and longing.

When you feel ready, read the psalm slowly, savouring the familiar words as if you had never read them before.

The reflection is in three parts. Each part works through several phrases of the psalm, with a summary word linked to each one. Pause at the end of each section to relate the thoughts to your own life experiences.

Part 1

'The Lord is my shepherd': Relationship

David was a shepherd himself and this psalm is a virtual handbook of shepherding practices. He watched over his flock in the hills around Bethlehem, the same area where, hundreds of years later, the shepherds saw the angels announcing the birth of Christ.

Shepherds were considered very lowly people, yet there are over 100 references to shepherds in scripture, perhaps because the qualities of shepherding make good metaphors for spiritual truths. For example, Jesus commissioned Peter to feed his lambs and look after his sheep (John 21:15–17).

There is a beautiful passage in Isaiah 40:11 which describes God as a tender shepherd: 'He tends his flock like a shepherd: he gathers the lambs in his arms and carries them close to his heart; he gently leads those that have young' (NIV).

Later, David was to be known as the shepherd-king. As a young man he would have spent many hours alone, looking after his flock of sheep. He knew each one and cared for them. It was on the hillsides of Judea that he developed his relationship with God and expressed that relationship in the music he played on his small harp and in the psalms he wrote. Some were of praise, some of lament, and some cried out to God in anguish and longing.

In Psalm 23, which so many of us know and love, David recognises that just as he was shepherd to his sheep, so the Lord was his shepherd. In different ways, each verse speaks of intimate relationship and dependency upon God.

You might want to pause and reflect on your own relationship with God. How was it formed? How has it developed? It is worth having a check-up because, if God is to refresh us and renew us in our relationship with him, then we have to ask what God means to us. In this psalm, David brings out some of God's most important attributes as he saw them.

'I shall not be in want': Supply

'My God will meet all your needs according to his glorious riches in Christ Jesus' (Philippians 4:19). These words were written by a man in prison for his faith and for his work in spreading the gospel. But Paul allowed God to supply his needs in that environment and was able to write confidently to his readers that God could do the same for them—and for us, his wider readership.

Jesus taught us to pray, 'Give us this day our daily bread' (Matthew 6:11)—not necessarily our chocolate cake but certainly our bread—all that we need to live life fully in his service with faith, hope, love and courage.

Just as the sheep under the shepherd's care do not suffer want, so we, when we put ourselves under God's care, will have all that we need to meet every situation.

'He makes me lie down in green pastures': Rest

The shepherd knew when to lead the sheep forward, and, in the Middle East at that time and still in many traditional cultures today, a shepherd leads the flock rather than following them. He knows when to let them rest. They need good grass to eat and a quiet place in which to lie down. Like us, sheep will not be able to rest if they are disturbed or anxious or hungry.

In another of David's psalms, he uses the same analogy of resting when he says, 'I will both lie down and sleep in peace; for you alone, O Lord, make me lie down in safety' (Psalm 4:8).

God knows, even if we don't, that we need periods of rest to recoup and renew our energy. That is why, as I mentioned at the very start of this book, periods of quiet reflection are so important, acting as punctuation marks in the prose of our lives, making sense of them.

'He leads me beside still waters': Refreshment

Sheep can survive in semi-arid land but they still need water, and the knowledge of where the water is lies with the shepherd. He knows where the drinking places are and he leads his flock to them. David is declaring that that is what God does for him, too.

Jesus said, 'Let anyone who is thirsty come to me and let the one who believes in me drink. As the scripture has said, "Out of the believer's heart shall flow rivers of living water"' (see John 7:37–38). The living water is the gift and work of God's Spirit, flowing in and through the lives of all who ask to receive.

Jesus also said to the Samaritan woman at the well:

If you knew the gift of God and who it is that is saying to you, 'Give me a drink', you would have asked him, and he would have given you living water... Everyone who drinks of this water [from the well] will be thirsty again, but those who drink of the water that I will give them will never be thirsty. The water that I will give will become in them a spring of water gushing up to eternal life. (John 4:10, 13–14)

To 'drink' in spiritual terms means to take in, to accept or to believe. It means to assimilate the life of God in Jesus to the point where it becomes part of us, just as water is assimilated into our body when we drink.

'He restores my soul': Healing

The soul is our interior life, the seat of our will and our emotions, the part of us that will outlast death and be clothed one day in a resurrection body.

In another of the psalms, the writer speaks to his own soul: 'Why are you cast down, O my soul, and why are you disquieted within me? Hope in God; for I shall again praise him, my help and my God' (Psalm 42:11).

In Psalm 23 we find David's answer to that cry. He opened his life to God so that eventually he was able to write, 'He restores my soul.' Such healing comes through God working together with us, and it may need to be a slow and gentle process. We might need to let him lead us back to memories of hurt, regret, rejection, failure or sadness and to revisit them, maybe with a trusted companion. We can face the pain and allow God to comfort us, forgive us or enable us to forgive others. This is a pathway to healing and restoration—a pathway that will allow us gradually to move on in our lives and in our relationship with God.

Relationship, supply, rest, refreshment, healing: these are the gifts that the Lord your Shepherd offers you.

Questions to ask yourself
In which situations have you found that God has given you what you needed in order to cope with them?

Are there any areas of your life where you feel that you need God's touch of healing and restoration? Find the time and the courage, and maybe a friend, to bring them to him.

A prayer

O Lord,
Set at rest the crowded, hurrying thoughts
within my mind and heart.
Let the peace and quiet of your presence
take full possession of me.

Help me to relax, to rest,
and to become open to yourself.

You know my inmost spirit,
the hidden unconscious life within me;
the forgotten memories of hurts and fears;
the frustrated desires;
the unresolved tensions;
the bewildering dilemmas.

Cleanse and sweeten the springs of my being,
that freedom, peace and love may flow
into both my conscious and my hidden inner life.

Lord,
I am open to your word,
I wait for your healing, and
I am more thankful for your presence with me
than anything else in the world.[1]

Part 2

'He leads me in right paths': Guidance

Sheep are notorious creatures of habit. They need careful managing and to be kept on the move, so that they do not overgraze their favourite spots and the vegetation is given a chance to recover. As David well knew, it would be an unintelligent and poor shepherd who would leave the sheep to fend completely for themselves. On the hills around Bethlehem, the sheep may have been prone to stray too far from the safety of the flock, and a shepherd was needed to keep an eye on them.

David was aware that God had guided him in good ways, even though occasionally he chose his own unwise path.

God wants to shepherd and guide us in the paths of righteousness, but we have to be open to his leading. Like sheep, we may prefer our own way. Isaiah writes, 'All we like sheep have gone astray; we have all turned to our own way' (Isaiah 53:6). God wants us all to move on with him. He wants us to walk with him, to stay close to him in obedience, to let him be our guide.

'For his name's sake': Purpose

God wants to lead us in good ways not only for our own well-being but also for his name's sake—his reputation and honour. God often gets bad publicity from us. When there are divisions between his people, a lack of generosity, harsh judgments or rampant selfishness, it does not reflect well on God. We say that we are Christians but sometimes we don't live it out.

God gives us a sense of purpose in our lives and will lead us in ways that are fulfilling, useful, compassionate and honouring to him. His desire is to use us in his service and bring glory rather than dishonour to him.

'Even though I walk through the darkest valley': Testing

Being led in God's ways does not mean that the road is always smooth. There are twists and turns in life. Sometimes it is hard going and demands some persistence. It can feel like walking through a dark valley, like being in a dark tunnel, unable to see any light at the end. I wonder if this has ever been your experience. We should remember, though, that 'no testing has overtaken you that is not common to everyone. God is faithful, and he will not let you be tested beyond your strength, but with the testing he will also provide the way out so that you may be able to endure it' (1 Corinthians 10:13).

Testing times can trouble us and cause us to be fearful, and David knew them in his own experience. For a considerable time he was constantly being hunted by King Saul, who wanted to kill him. Living rough and in hiding, in fear for his life, he would have known what it was to walk through a dark valley (in other translations, 'the valley of the shadow of death) but he could declare confidently the next phrase of the psalm.

'I fear no evil': Protection

In Psalm 27, David writes:

The Lord is my light and my salvation; whom shall I fear? The Lord is the stronghold of my life; of whom shall I be afraid? When evildoers assail me to devour my flesh—my adversaries and foes—

they shall stumble and fall. Though an army encamp against me,
my heart shall not fear; though war rise up against me, yet will I be
confident. (Psalm 27:1–3)

This was David's experience. He faced huge threats to his life, such as we will probably never have to face, so why can he say that he will not be afraid? The answer comes in the next phrase of Psalm 23.

'For you are with me': Faithfulness

It is interesting to note that the pronoun in the psalm has changed from 'he' to 'you', which gives a sense of greater intimacy. 'You, Lord, are with me in dark and challenging times. I don't just know it as a fact in my head but in the experience of my heart,' David could have said.

God is faithful. He does not abandon us in our difficulties. He may not change the circumstances but he will give us what we need to live without fear and in an attitude of trust. Often, it is when difficult circumstances bring us to a low point that we encounter God. In fact, sometimes he trusts us with a sense of his absence rather than his presence. This can lead to a deeper maturity as we learn to rely less on 'feeling' his presence. He is true to his word and will not abandon us or leave us as orphans (John 14:18).

'Your rod and your staff comfort me': Reassurance

In the Middle East, a shepherd of David's time carried only a rod and a staff. The rod was like an extension of the shepherd's arm: it was usually a thick stick with a knob at the end, like a cudgel. He used it to protect himself and his flock from the wild animals that roamed the hills of Judea. Listen to the young David telling King Saul about his experiences: 'Your servant used to keep sheep for his father; and whenever a lion or a bear came, and took a lamb from the flock, I went after it and struck it down, rescuing the lamb from its mouth; and if it turned against me, I would catch it by the jaw, strike it down, and kill it' (1 Samuel 17:34–35).

The shepherd would also have used the rod to bring into line any wayward sheep that had wandered away. Sometimes he would throw the rod just beyond the wandering sheep to send the animal scurrying back to the flock. The rod conveyed the idea of power and authority, discipline and defence.

The staff, however, speaks of kindness. It was normally a long slender stick, often with a crook or a hook at one end, that could be used in several ways. It could be used to lift a newborn lamb gently and bring it to its mother if they had become separated. That way, the shepherd avoided transferring the smell of his hands on to the lamb, which might make the mother reject it.

He would use it, too, to catch hold of an individual sheep to examine it. Sometimes he would walk alongside a sheep that needed encouraging, gently keeping the staff in touch with the sheep's side—a sort of holding hands. This would be a comfort and reassurance for the sheep.

The word 'comfort' stems from *con*, meaning 'with', and *fortis*, meaning 'strength'.

That was David's experience when he found himself in hard places: God would come alongside him with strength. In this psalm, although David was a shepherd, he speaks from the point of view of the sheep, on the receiving end of shepherding.

God offers us his guidance, purpose, protection, faithfulness and reassurance, especially in times of testing. Are you in need of any of these gifts in your life as it is now?

Your security lies not in your environment, whether green pastures and still waters or the darkest valley, but in your Shepherd. With him there is neither want nor fear.

Questions to ask yourself
Think back over your life. In what ways has God guided you, whether you were aware of it or not at the time?

Let situations of anxiety, loss, illness, confusion or depression come to mind. How did you experience God's help and comfort? If you didn't, what do you think might have been blocking the experience?

Prayer

O Lord, you can only lead when I will follow.
Help me to trust you in all things and at all times—
you, who know the end from the beginning.

Part 3

'You prepare a table before me': Hope

The scene has changed. In David's imagination, he is no longer out of doors but indoors; no longer a sheep in a flock, but a guest at a banquet. His divine host has prepared a table before him. What a different picture from the dark valley! This is full of hope and provision and celebration. It is not a secret feast but is enjoyed in full view.

'In the presence of my enemies': Strength

When God satisfies the soul, it cannot be hidden from the world. He fills us with strength and a love that is evident to others.

God lavished his love on us and, at great cost to himself, prepared a special table that we can call the Lord's Table. He invites us to eat the bread and drink the wine, symbols of the great sacrifice that Jesus made on our behalf when he gave his body to be crucified and shed his blood for us so that we might have peace with God and become inheritors of his eternal kingdom. The Passover feast that became the Last Supper was arranged while Jesus was surrounded by enemies and was eaten only hours before his arrest.

'You anoint my head with oil': Consecration

David had the experience of being anointed and consecrated as the future king by Samuel: 'Samuel took the horn of oil and anointed him in the presence of his brothers; and the spirit of the Lord came mightily upon David from that day forward' (1 Samuel 16:13).

As well as being a sign of dedication to God, anointing a head with perfumed oil was the customary treatment given to an honoured guest, which is what Psalm 23 specifically refers to here. God has bestowed his blessing and honour on each of us. He consecrates us in his service. So lift up your head and listen to the words of John in his letter: 'You have been anointed by the Holy One, and all of you have knowledge' (1 John 2:20). We are not only the honoured guests at the Lord's table; we are also his dedicated servants, set apart to be his representatives to others.

'And my cup overflows': Abundance

Jesus said, 'I came that they may have life, and have it abundantly' (John 10:10). We do not have a stingy God but a generous one. We can never outgive God: he wants to give us more and more. He desires to fill us to the brim and running over with his blessings, if we will but receive them.

'Surely goodness and love...': Blessing

The fact is that God longs to bless us with his goodness and his love, not occasionally but always, for his blessing is lifelong.

'... will follow me all the days of my life': Promise

Can we really believe, like David, that no matter what happens in our lives, we are being followed by goodness and love ('and mercy' in the King James Version)?

David says '*Surely…*'. It is certain, without a doubt. He also says that goodness and love *will* follow him. There is no wishful thinking here. It is a promise that he is trusting for *all* the days of his life, and he says, '… *my* life' because what he says is not just a fact for others but a lived experience for himself.

I remember an old chorus with the words 'Count your blessings, name them one by one, and it will surprise you what the Lord has done.' At a time of quiet reflection, it is a good idea to gather together instances of God's blessing in your life, and then remember them with thankfulness.

'And I shall dwell in the house of the Lord': Security

God offers us a home, a place of security.

When David spoke of 'the house of the Lord', he would probably have had in mind the temple or the tabernacle, places that represented God's presence on earth.

Through Jesus, we can extend this thought. Listen to some astonishing words spoken by him to his disciples on the eve of his death: 'Those who love me will keep my word, and my Father will love them, and we will come to them and make our home with them' (John 14:23).

A little later, he said, 'Abide in me as I abide in you' (John 15:4), or, in other words, 'Make your home in me and I will make mine in you.'

Our loving, merciful, faithful Father and Jesus Christ his Son want to share our interior soul-home, not just in this life but for all eternity.

'For ever': Eternity

We have the consolation of Jesus' words on the last night of his earthly life: 'In my Father's house there are many dwelling-places. If it were not so, would I have told you that I go to prepare a place for you? And if I go and prepare a place for you, I will come again and will take you to myself, so that where I am, you may be also' (John 14:2–3).

God offers us an eternal home, not because we have earned it—we never could—but because Jesus has made it available to us through his redeeming love and his sacrificial death.

One day we will see God face to face and there will be a grand reunion. Perhaps we will meet David the shepherd-king there, too.

Hope, strength, consecration, abundance, blessing, promise. security and eternity: what more can we ask for? How foolish of us to live impoverished lives when, all the time, there are so many blessings of God at our disposal!

For reflection

Jesus said, 'You did not choose me but I chose you. And I appointed you to go and bear fruit, fruit that will last' (John 15:16).

As we have seen, God has anointed each of us to serve him in our own style, through our own unique personality and in our own set of circumstances. Can you think of ways in which God uses you to shepherd others of any age and in whatever context?

Are there any lessons to be learned from the way the Lord shepherds his people?

You might like to write Psalm 23 in your own words, using situations that are relevant to you.

If you have a musical setting of Psalm 23, this would be a good time to play it, to close the time of reflection.

Blessing

May the God of peace, who through the blood of the eternal covenant brought back from the dead our Lord Jesus, that great Shepherd of the sheep, equip you with everything good for doing his will, and may he work in us what is pleasing to him, through Jesus Christ, to whom be glory for ever and ever. Amen (Hebrews 13:20–21)

A time for change

For this reflection, it would be helpful to have some leaves that are beginning to turn from green into their autumn colours.

The reflection is in two parts and develops the theme of change and transition that we all experience from time to time in our lives.

Part 1: Winds of change

September is not quite summer and not quite autumn, as the autumn equinox falls around 23 September, when the length of daytime and night-time are equal. During this month we see the full 'harvest moon', so named because it gave extra light to the farmers struggling to bring in their crops before the advent of tractors and combine-harvesters, with their powerful headlights.

Trees are just beginning to change colour and, in a month or so, they will lose their leaves. There is a change in the weather. Nights are cooler and it becomes dark a little earlier. Even the light is changing: when the sun shines, it seems golden. September can offer us some of the most beautiful of days. If we have had a disappointing summer, then the warm, hazy days of September are welcome and are often called an 'Indian summer'.

Nature will shortly begin its preparations for the harsh conditions of winter. Even though there is beauty all around us, the year is in transition and change is everywhere.

Throughout the course of our own lives, we too experience changes. Some are minor and hardly noticed; others are major and cause serious upheaval. Life is never static: how boring it would be if it was! There is usually some kind of change going on: something new is happening to us all the time. It is fundamental to the human condition that we live with change.

We have all arrived where we are today because of a series of changes:

- From the womb to the shock of birth.
- From babyhood to becoming independent little beings who feed ourselves, walk and communicate.
- From being at home to going to school and learning new skills.
- At puberty our bodies undergo changes and lead us to sexual maturity.
- Then can follow college, university, apprenticeship or getting a job, which perhaps gives us financial independence.
- A big change occurs if we join our life to another's in marriage or some form of commitment. This calls for adjustments, and presents many challenges as well as joys and blessings.
- From being 'the two of us' to becoming parents is another major change to negotiate.
- The cycle begins again, but we are a generation on, and there are more changes to face because there are more family members who closely affect our lives, including ageing parents and children who eventually leave home, emptying the nest.
- Women's bodies undergo another change at the time of the menopause and they enter a different phase in life.

- There is a change from the workplace to retirement, with new possibilities but also big adjustments.
- Then comes the challenge of the ageing process, which is not easy for us. Having been independent for most of our lives, we may have to face the prospect of being dependent once more.
- Ultimately we face death, which is a passage to new life.

Some changes are probably under our control, such as our choice of a career, a partner, a home and location, a job change or retirement. Some changes are thrust upon us, such as a move in childhood because of a parent's change of job, the separation or divorce of parents, being faced with bereavement, being depended on for care or becoming ill or incapacitated in some way ourselves, which brings restrictions to our lifestyle.

Some changes are marked by external events, such as the birth of a child or grandchild, children leaving home, a house move, a change of job or a new role. Other changes are invisible, happening within us—maybe a change of attitude; a decision to forgive someone who has hurt us, which releases us to move on; fresh inspiration or revelation, which can be life-changing.

Of course, changes don't arrive singly. We may move through several at once, but in all cases we enter uncharted territory. Inevitably, change brings some kind of upheaval. At the same time, a right degree of stress can be helpful to us because it acts as a stimulus and a challenge.

Whether the changes are chosen by us or imposed on us, whether they are outer or inner, they are not only social and psychological changes but passages of the Spirit too.

Whether the changes feel good or bad, we can encounter God in the midst of them, for God is always found within human experience. Our lives are known to him. He loves and cares for us.

Sometimes we are very aware of his presence, his comfort and strength, his communication. At other times, as we have reflected elsewhere in this book, he trusts us with his seeming absence. This does not mean that he is absent but, rather, that we don't have a sense of his presence. We can feel that he has abandoned us and think that perhaps it is because of our own fault.

The psalmist writes, 'Why, O Lord, do you stand far off? Why do you hide yourself in times of trouble'? (Psalm 10:1). He feels that his enemies are triumphing over him, but, at the end of the psalm, he declares, 'You hear, O Lord, the desire of the afflicted; you encourage them, and you listen to their cry' (v. 17, NIV). When we feel that God is far off, it is an opportunity to trust him and to be patient. The psalmist speaks again: 'I wait for the Lord, my soul waits, and in his word I hope' (Psalm 130:5). God knows what will help us through change and into growth, whether it is a definite awareness of his presence or giving us the space in which to grow up.

In the days following the resurrection, the disciples experienced a lot of absence. Jesus would come briefly and then leave them for a while. Although they needed comfort and reassurance, he knew, too, that they needed space to process what was going on and to let their faith develop further. He gave them just enough of his presence to lead them on. It was his way of loving them into renewal and courage to face the future without his physical presence.

For reflection

Try to identify some of the changes that have occurred in your life.

- What was it that triggered them?
- What stress did you experience at the time and what were the feelings associated with it?
- What has resulted from the changes—a fresh direction, new friendships, a different role or new skills?

Are there any changes that you are facing now, or any that you know you are likely to face in the future? What might be the consequences?

Prayer

O Lord, with whom there is no shadow of turning,
our constancy in times of change,
hold us steady when we feel uncertain;
comfort and embolden us when we feel afraid;
open our eyes to new possibilities and fresh direction;
help us to step out into the unknown,
confident to face the future with you,
who in your love gave your life for us. Amen

Part 2: From one season to another

Change and transition are two different things.

Change is concerned mainly with external circumstances—for example, the birth of a child, a job loss, the death of a loved one, a house move or retirement.

Transition is the passage in between the endings and the new beginnings—a period between the old and the new. Sometimes it is protracted and sometimes it is very short.

Transition, therefore, is the emotional and spiritual process that we go through in coming to terms with change. We have to be honest with ourselves to decide what we need to do to manage this process well. Our differing temperaments will affect the way we respond to change and the period of transition. I was talking to two friends the other evening about the subject of change. One woman said, 'I love change.' The other said, 'I don't do change. I don't like change.' They admitted that they were like chalk and cheese, very different in temperament.

Also, of course, the particular nature of the change makes a difference to the way we manage it. Celebrating a job promotion with all the changes it will entail is very different from experiencing the loss of a close relative.

Think of the disciples after the crucifixion and burial of Jesus, when they were all crowded together in a locked room for fear of further persecution. I guess that, because of our human differences, there would have been a range of emotional responses among the disciples. Some may have become silent and morose, turned in on themselves. Others would have needed to express their grief by talking about it, going over and over the events. Some may have paced restlessly; others perhaps expressed their grief in tears or by escaping into sleep. There was probably a lot of edginess and confusion. It was not an easy time to be huddled together, afraid of what might happen to them. Into this highly charged atmosphere Jesus came, standing among them and greeting them with 'Peace be with you.'

We, too, in the uncertainty of change or loss, can experience some of the same emotions that the disciples endured—withdrawal, restlessness, fear, anger, depression and anxiety. And, like the disciples, we can experience Jesus' loving presence bringing us peace.

I recently talked to a man who had just come out of a second period of redundancy. The first time, he had not been a Christian and he said that it had been a horrendous experience. He had felt very unsure of himself, and his confidence had dropped to an all-time low as panic set in.

Facing redundancy again, but now as a Christian, he found that although it had not been easy, he had had a real experience of God 'holding' him and a sense that God knew his situation. He had begun to trust God for the future and, with his family's support, had been able to take the knocks of refusals to job applications, cancelled appointments and the rejection of being turned down.

In every experience there is a gift. In this case, because no money was coming in, his wife had had to take a job, which she was very much enjoying, and would continue even though her husband had now found work. With their mother having less time at home, the two teenage children now had to help with the work of looking after their home, so there was growth all round. The family has come through the experience stronger, more bonded, wiser and, I think, better equipped for future changes. They have trusted God and found him faithful.

Here are some points to consider in relation to transition. You may find it helpful to go through each one in turn and think about how they might apply to your own situation. Writing your thoughts down will give you more understanding of what is going on.

1 Reaffirm your trust in God and give priority to your relationship with him.
2 Acknowledge what losses are involved for you in the transition.
3 Ask what you should celebrate from what has been.
4 Ask yourself what you will be taking with you into the new chapter of life—lessons learnt, new skills or more wisdom, perhaps.
5 Begin to let go. It is the pattern of nature that for the regeneration of plants to take place, seeds drop, lie dormant, germinate and then produce new growth. It is the pattern of each day. The sun sets and darkness takes over through night until dawn and the breaking of a new day. Transition always begins with an ending.
6 Wait; be patient with yourself. Jesus had to wait until he was 30 years old before starting his ministry; Paul, that man of action and energy, had to wait three years in the Arabian desert before he was ready for the work that God had for him; the disciples had to wait 50 days after the resurrection until Pentecost, when the Holy Spirit came to them and they could move into fresh ministry. We tend to want to move quickly from the old to the new, but this is not possible, because transition is a journey from one identity to another. That takes time.

7   Dare to give voice to any questions that lie within you. Now can be a time to reassess. Are there ways in which God may want to change not only your circumstances but you as well? Do you have any attitudes that need to change or any area of unforgiveness that you need to release, in order to move on?

8   Try to find a network of support and understanding. This is a time when family, friends and the church family can come alongside you.

9   Take the risk required to move on. The desire to hold on to the familiar is entirely understandable, however stressful and difficult, but to move on into the unknown requires risk and trust in God.

10 Turn to embrace the new. Grace will be given for the next season of life by God, who knows you and loves you. In the change lie seeds of growth and new possibilities.

An exercise

Take a piece of A4 paper and draw four sections.

- Take a few moments to think of an issue that is concerning you, one that will involve change. Let an image of it come to mind and then draw it in the top left section. (Don't worry if you can only draw stick men!)

- In your imagination, project forward to what might happen as a result of the change and draw it in the top right section.

- Ask yourself what the hindrances might be to moving or making the change. In the bottom left section, draw an image to represent what comes to mind.

- Finally, take time to pray and to ask God for his perspective—his bigger picture—and draw what you thought of in the remaining section.

Reflect on the moods and images that came to you while doing this exercise and bring them to God in prayer.

Prayer

In the uncertainty of transition and in times of change,
'Show me your ways, O Lord,
teach me your paths.
Guide me in your truth and teach me,
for you are God my Saviour,
and my hope is in you all day long.'
PSALM 25:4–5 (NIV)

Autumn

For this opening meditation, you will need a Bible open at 2 Corinthians 5:1–10 and some music, perhaps 'Autumn' from Vivaldi's *The Four Seasons*.

- Find a quiet place and sit or kneel in a relaxed posture.
- Allow all tension to drain away; slow your breathing until it is deeper. Be aware of the incoming and outgoing breaths. Relax.
- Affirm God's loving presence and commit yourself to him, saying, 'In the name of the Father and of the Son and of the Holy Spirit.'
- Read 2 Corinthians 5:1–10 slowly and reflectively. It speaks of the supreme and certain hope that when our earthly life is over, we will be clothed with a heavenly body and enjoy the miracle of new and eternal life in the presence of God.
- Listen to Vivaldi's 'Autumn' or other suitable music.
- Open yourself to the thoughts of the passage, allowing the Holy Spirit to take you where he will.
- Emerge gently from the meditation and give thanks to God for his goodness, love and guidance.

The following is a reflection on autumn in three parts, which can be used together or separately.

It is hard to know which is my favourite season of the year, but it is probably a toss-up between spring and autumn. I appreciate the freshness and the sharp colours of spring, the lime and yellow and hyacinth blue with splashes of pink blossom. But I also take delight in the colours of fire and the bright-berried hedgerows of autumn. Autumn begins in September and ends in November. Some people feel that autumn is a sad month because so much is dying, however gloriously, but there is also a sense in which autumn is the climax of the year, abounding in fruitfulness.

Our summer bird visitors are leaving us for warmer climes, and who can blame them? It is estimated that 5000 million land birds migrate from Europe to Africa each autumn, but there is also an exchange, as flocks of birds, mostly larger ones, fly in from northern and eastern Europe to winter here in our comparatively warm islands.

There is so much beauty in autumn. The heavy falls of dew, resulting from cool air meeting the still warm earth, spangle the spiders' webs and silver the grass; trees are aflame, dressed in butter gold, russet, dazzling vermilion and crimson; on a gusty day the leaves whirl and dance in the wind before falling to the ground; when the frost arrives, it edges each fallen leaf with white crystals. At sunset, autumn skies are often flushed with colours ranging from indigo and violet to warm peach and slashes of red.

It is not only a beautiful season of the year but it also has its own particular scents: the musky smell of weird and wonderful fungi that push their way through layers of rotten woodland past; the aroma of bonfires as piles of rubbish and prunings are burnt, after a great garden clear-up; the smell of the dank earth and freshly fallen leaves drenched by rain.

It is a season of much change as the year moves from the warm, balmy, golden days of early September to the cooler air that brings mists, fog and frost in October and November. There is work to do on the land—ploughing and sowing winter wheat. Gardeners are busy 'putting their gardens to bed', which involves tidying up, clearing, cutting down, composting, sweeping up the leaves and perhaps planting bulbs for spring colour.

There are several themes relating to the season of autumn that could form the basis for reflection. I have chosen three which you may like to look at together or use on separate occasions:

- Fruitfulness
- Letting go
- Ageing

Part 1: A season of fruitfulness

It was John Keats who began his poem 'Ode to Autumn' (1819) with these lines:

> *Season of mists and mellow fruitfulness!*
> *Close bosom-friend of the maturing sun;*
> *Conspiring with him how to load and bless*
> *With fruit the vines that round the thatch-eaves run;*
> *To bend with apples the moss'd cottage trees,*
> *And fill all fruit with ripeness to the core...*

Trees in the orchards are laden with apples and pears; there are nuts on the hazel bushes; shiny, brown conkers lie on the ground, asking to be picked up; sloes, hips and haws, elderberries and juicy blackberries lace the hedgerows; mushrooms litter the woodland floor and many people go out to make the most of them. We store the fruits, freeze them, bottle them, make wine out of them, and turn them into chutneys, jellies and jam. We cook exotic wild mushroom risottos or fruit crumbles.

It is not just we human beings who enjoy all this bounty, but squirrels, fieldmice, birds and butterflies will find ways to use the fruits. The squirrels hide what nuts and acorns they can find, banking them for hungrier times ahead. Butterflies feast on the fallen, rotting apples and pears, while the birds and mice colonise the hedgerows, where food is abundant in berry and seed. When the birds roost at night, it is like sleeping in a larder! They will need all the sustenance they can get, to build up their reserves before the onset of winter. God is faithful and each year the bountiful goodness of creation is available to us, part of the pattern of nature's cycle.

In Luke 6:43–45 Jesus spoke to a gathered crowd about fruitfulness. He said:

No good tree bears bad fruit, nor again does a bad tree bear good fruit; for each tree is known by its own fruit. Figs are not gathered from thorns, nor are grapes picked from a bramble bush. The good person out of the good treasure of the heart produces good, and the evil person out of evil treasure produces evil; for it is out of the abundance of the heart that the mouth speaks.'

Here, the fruit is the words that we speak, which come from our thoughts and emotions—the treasure of our hearts, as Jesus puts it, whether it be good and kind or bitter and destructive.

In Matthew 13:1–23, Jesus left the house where he was staying, probably at Capernaum, and walked to the edge of the lake to sit and pray. As usual, though, it did not take long for crowds to gather around him. He did not chide them for interrupting the precious time he had to himself. Instead he got into a boat and pushed a little way from the shore, and from that watery pulpit he taught the people, using parables.

Perhaps, from his vantage point, he saw a farmer sowing seed on his newly ploughed land, and he used it as a visual aid for a parable that would get to the core of how they would respond to his words about the kingdom of God. He likened people's lives to four kinds of soil. Some were like a well-compacted path beside the field, where the seed would never germinate but would become food for the birds; others like rocky ground where, although the seed would take root, because the soil was shallow the plants would die in the fierce sun, as their roots were not deep enough and could not find moisture in the shallow soil. Some of the soil in which the seed landed was in the midst of thorns and thistles, which grew alongside the seed and eventually choked it. The seed that produced the fruit that God was looking for fell on fertile ground, which not only gave a good yield but also produced seed for future sowings.

For reflection

From verse18 onwards, Jesus interprets the parable for the disciples, and therein lie challenges for each of us as we think about the soil of our lives and what grows there.

Which of the four growing conditions most often typifies your life?

In John 15:1–17, we hear Jesus speaking to his friends just hours before his arrest. He likens himself to the true vine and us to the branches, while his Father is the vine grower. A vine exists to bear fruit through its branches, and the fruit that Jesus is speaking of is the fruit of love—an outward expression of the life of God within us, which will always reveal itself through compassion and other good characteristics, as described by Paul in his letter to the Galatians (5:22–23): 'The fruit of the Spirit is love, joy, peace, patience, kindness, generosity, faithfulness, gentleness, and self-control.'

This is the fruit that God is looking for, and it will grow naturally as an expression of our life in Christ. Just as the vine draws up goodness through its roots from the soil, and the sap carries it into the branches, so Jesus' own life nurtures us—we who are the branches. How vital, then, that we stay connected to Jesus and so produce fruit that is a result of his life in God!

Part 2: Letting go

You only have to say the word 'autumn', and immediately images of vivid colours come to mind—red, orange, yellow and crimson—as trees and shrubs put on a magnificent display for us. Their leaves die in an unsurpassed blaze of glory. It was many years before I questioned how it all happened and why the leaves turned from green into the vibrant colours of their autumn dress. Here follows a brief botany lesson, with apologies to those who know it already!

- Leaves provide plants and trees with the food they need to survive.
- Trees take in water from the ground through their roots. They also take in carbon dioxide from the air. Sunlight is used to turn the water and carbon dioxide into a sugar called glucose, which is what trees feed on. This process is called photosynthesis.
- Leaves also contain a green chemical called chlorophyll. This helps with photosynthesis and gives the leaves their colour, but chlorophyll is not the only coloured pigment in the leaf. There are other pigments—the carotenes and xanthophylls, which are yellow and orange—but these colours are usually masked by the green of the chlorophyll.
- In autumn, the chlorophyll in the leaf begins to break down and the yellow, orange and red pigments, which were there all the time, begin to show through.
- In winter, there is not enough sunlight for the trees to make food. The leaves are no longer useful and, in fact, a tree in leaf is at greater risk of damage in a winter gale, so the tree gets rid of them.

- The leaf stem is sealed off from the branch. The stems become weaker and the leaves can easily be blown away in a gust of wind, leaving just the bare branches that we see in winter.

On a windy day in October, I like to walk in beech woods and watch the leaves come fluttering and spiralling down to rest on the woodland floor. I try to imagine what it would be like to be a leaf, bursting from its protective calyx in the spring, unfurling and unfolding, limp at first but then strengthened by the food it receives from the sun and the rain; fluttering in the breezes of summer; held still on languid, hot days; observing the birds and squirrels that nest, hide and take shelter in the trees; having its food supply cut off in the autumn until one day, as a result of a weakened stem and a gust of wind, the leaf lets go and descends from its lofty perch to the ground below. There it will be broken down by bacteria until it rots and adds its nutrients to the humus, which in turn will nourish the tree on which it once grew and had life.

Autumn is a necessary transition between the fruitfulness of summer and the new life of spring. No new growth will come unless autumn agrees to let go of what has been. It is the same in our lives. We cannot grow and develop without change. Life events that tear at our securities are like dying leaves. We would prefer to cling to the known, even though it might be unhappy and far from life-giving. But when we surrender to the process of change, rather than running away from it in fear, growth will happen and new possibilities will open up.

A prayer for autumn days

God of the seasons, there is a time for everything; there is a time for dying and rising. We need courage to enter into the transformation process.

God of autumn, the trees are saying goodbye to their green, letting go of what has been. We, too, have our moments of surrender, with all their insecurity and risk. Help us to let go where we need to do so.

God of fallen leaves lying in coloured patterns on the ground, our lives have their own patterns. As we see the patterns of our own growth, may we learn from them.

God of misty days and harvest moon nights, there is always the dimension of mystery and wonder in our lives. We always need to recognise your power-filled presence. May we gain strength from you.

God of orchards and fields of ripened grain, many gifts of growth lie in the season of our surrender. We must wait for harvest in faith and hope. Grant us patience when we do not see the blessings.

God of birds flying south for another season, your wisdom enables us to know what needs to be left behind and what needs to be carried into the future. We need your insight and vision.

God of flowers touched with frost and windows wearing white designs, may your love keep our hearts from growing cold in the empty seasons.

God of life, you believe in us, you enrich us, you entrust us with the freedom to choose life.

For all this we are grateful.[1]

Part 3: Ageing

By the time autumn arrives, the plants that showed such vigour and freshness in spring and summer are looking tired and many have drooped. The lambs and the fledglings have grown to maturity. The warm air is giving way to a chill, which can bring frost and cold. It seems that ageing is taking place in nature, and often we think of autumn as an image of ageing in our lives, too.

But it is not all doom and gloom, because autumn and the ageing process both have much to offer, and I write from experience! True, we slow down, stiffen up and have less energy than we used to have; hearing and eyesight can become less effective and general repairs may be needed here and there, but there are compensations. In theory, we have more time to use and to be still, and what time we have is free from many of the structures that were once imposed on it.

We may feel released from the pressure to justify ourselves or fulfil other people's expectations. It has been my experience that as people grow older, they become more truly themselves. The need to control starts to slip away and there is nothing to prove to yourself and others. I remember talking to an elderly retired bishop. He was quite content in his decision to leave the public arena and to be more at rest and at prayer, preparing himself for the greatest adventure of all, beyond death.

Even if our bodies are full of aches and pains, our soul need not grow old; it remains youthful and strong if we allow it to be. Instead of seeing ourselves as in decline, we can hold the ideal aloft that we are in a process of growth, emotionally and spiritually, even if our physical powers diminish. As our outer life slows down, our inner life can become more important and enriched. Paul picks up this idea in 2 Corinthians 4:16: 'So we do not lose heart. Even though our outer nature is wasting away, our inner nature is being renewed day by day.'

I had a dear friend, the same age as me, who contracted motor neuron disease, which meant that although her mental faculties were intact, her body was packing up and becoming useless to her. She lived in New Zealand and, three months before she died, I went with my husband to visit her. She could no longer speak or use any part of her body, but she could still smile and she could grunt, so that if you held a card with letters of the alphabet in front of her, she would make a sound when you pointed to the one that added to the spelling of the word that she wanted to communicate.

Despite the appalling limitations in her life, she seemed to be at peace. She was a committed Christian and loved her Lord, from whom she was receiving such grace to live each day. Before I left, I remember saying to her, 'Sally, though your body may have let you down, nothing can touch your inner life with God, and I sense that that is being renewed and growing day by day.' She rewarded me with a beautiful smile, which I will never forget, because she knew it to be true.

God is with us and his desire is to set us free, even within the limitations imposed on us by the ageing process—free to develop deeper relationships with himself and others, free to reflect on all that life has been and free to delve into our treasury of memories. As John O'Donohue writes, 'Old age is a time of coming home to your deeper nature, of entering fully into the temple of your memory where all your vanished days are secretly gathered awaiting you.'[2]

Again we turn for consolation and challenge to the letters of Paul: '[The Lord] said to me, "My grace is sufficient for you, for power is made perfect in weakness." So, I will boast all the more gladly of my weaknesses, so that the power of Christ may rest in me' (2 Corinthians 12:9).

Some questions to consider
- What is less important to me now than earlier in life?
- What is more important to me now than earlier in life?
- What are some of my most treasured memories?
- What causes my soul to sing?

The righteous flourish like the palm tree,
and grow like a cedar in Lebanon.
They are planted in the house of the Lord;
they flourish in the courts of our God.
In old age they still produce fruit;
they are always green and full of sap,
showing that the Lord is upright. (Psalm 92:12–15)

Prayer

O God, we thank you for the gift of years; for the opportunity to see the pattern of our lives and to have experienced the deaths from which we have risen over and over again. As we continue our journey, give us lightness of step and lightness of heart that we may grace our world with a spirit of joy and gratitude. We ask this in the name of Jesus who has gone before and continues to walk the way with us. Amen[3]

Open hands

As an aid to meditation, if possible have a quiet piece of instrumental music ready to be played.

The hand is a masterly creation of intricate design. With bones for strength and joints for flexibility, with the positioning of the thumb, the tendons and the movement of the muscles, we are able to grasp large objects and pick up tiny ones. The nails offer protection for this valuable tool and the fingertips contain some of the densest areas of nerve endings in the body, which means that they are able to give the brain instant feedback through their sensitivity to hot, cold, wet and dry conditions, and to what is hard, soft or sharp.

Next to our eyes, our hands are probably the most expressive part of us. They provide us with a means of communication and a tool to work with. They can be used for good in giving, building and loving, or for ill in stealing, destroying and abusing.

In R.S. Thomas' poem 'The hand', he imagines God having a struggle with himself as he creates the first hand, knowing what things it will be capable of. He ends with the lines:

Messenger to the mixed things
of your making, tell them I am.[1]

Read through the next four points, then put the book aside and focus on this stilling exercise.

- Sit in a relaxed position, taking time to let any tension in your body disappear.
- Place your hands with palms down on your lap as you gradually let go of all that concerns you, in order to create space for you and God.
- Turn your palms upwards as a symbol of emptiness, openness, a willingness to receive but also of vulnerability.
- Cup your hands as you sense that God holds you—gently, as you would hold a small bird in your hand, not tightly so that it would be crushed, and not with open hands so that it feels unsafe, but securely held.

Reflect on these words: 'The eternal God is your refuge, and underneath are the everlasting arms' (Deuteronomy 33:27, NIV).

Play your piece of music and enjoy the awareness of being open and receptive to the one who holds you.

The hands of Jesus

Use your imagination to picture the hands of Jesus at different stages in his life. Let the images unfold slowly, one by one, in your mind's eye.

- A newborn baby, his fingers curled around Mary's finger. His hands are perfectly formed but he is unable to do anything for himself. He is God in human form, helpless and totally dependent on others.

- A child at play, learning to write or helping in the home.
- A young man alongside his father, working with wood, repairing and constructing.
- In the desert, where for 40 days and nights he was tempted by Satan. He used his hands to pick up and turn over a stone as he struggled with the thought of using his power to turn it into bread to satisfy his hunger.
- Reaching out to heal—touching eyes, unstopping ears, rebuking fever, delivering from evil spirits, taking hold of a little girl's hand and raising her to life again.
- Using his hands expressively as he told stories or to emphasise a point when teaching the crowds.
- Stretching out his hands over rough waters to calm a storm.
- Helping Peter, who was sinking, up out of the water and back into the boat.
- Using his hands to wash and dry his disciples' feet, to demonstrate that he had come to serve rather than to be served.
- At the last supper with his disciples, when he took the bread and the wine, symbols of his own body and blood, blessed them and shared them around.
- Pleading with his Father in the garden of Gethsemane, feeling anguish about the death that he knew faced him.
- Having his hands bound and tied behind his back while he was whipped and spat upon.
- Carrying his cross, feeling the weight and the roughness of it.
- Feeling the searing pain, the nails tearing into his wrists, severing the tendons, as the Son of God was crucified.
- Straining to speak out his final words, 'Father, into your hands I commit my spirit.'

- The white, lifeless hands of Jesus as he was wrapped in a shroud and laid in a borrowed tomb.
- Appearing to the disciples on the first evening of his resurrection, raising a hand in the traditional greeting of shalom—peace be with you. He showed them his scarred hands and feet as proof that it really was him.
- Inviting Thomas to touch his hands and feet, so that his disciple might not doubt but believe that he had indeed risen from the dead.
- Cooking breakfast for his disciples on the shore of Lake Galilee in one of his resurrection appearances.
- Blessing the bread and giving thanks to his Father, revealing himself as the risen Jesus to two disciples with whom he had walked to Emmaus.
- Gesturing and giving instructions to his disciples to go into the world and preach the gospel.
- Leading his disciples to a hill top, blessing them with uplifted hands and, in the act of blessing, departing from them.
- Now seated in majesty at the right hand of God.

Jesus lived his life generously and with open hands.

A story

In a tiny village in Nuremberg, Germany, in the 15th century, there lived a family with 18 children. In order to feed his family, Albrecht Dürer the Elder worked all hours of the day at his goldsmith's trade.

Despite their poverty, two of his sons had a dream. They were both artistic, having learnt the art of engraving from their father. They wanted to study art at the Nuremberg Academy, but knew that the family finances would never stretch to affording the fees.

After many talks together late into the night, the two sons came up with a plan. They would toss a coin and the loser would work in the nearby mines to pay for his brother to attend the academy. After the winner had completed his four years of studies, he would support the other brother, either by the sale of his artwork or by also working down the mines.

They tossed the coin on a Sunday morning after church. The young Albrecht won the toss and went off to study at the Academy. He was highly talented and his work there was an immediate success. By the time he graduated, he was beginning to earn considerable fees for his commissioned works.

When Albrecht returned to his village, the family held a festive dinner to celebrate his homecoming. At the end of the meal, young Albrecht rose from his chair at the head of the table and asked the guests to drink a toast to his beloved brother as a way of thanking him for all the years of sacrifice that had allowed him to study. 'And now, Albert, blessed brother of mine, it is your turn. You can now go to the Academy and I will support you.'

But Albert, at the far end of the table, sat with tears streaming down his face. Eventually he stood to reply: 'No, brother. I cannot go to Nuremberg. It is too late for me. Look what four years down the mines have done to my hands. The bones in my fingers have been smashed and, just lately, I have been suffering from arthritis in my right hand. I cannot even hold a glass to return your toast, and would not be able to hold a pen or a brush to make delicate lines on parchment. No, brother, for me it is too late.'

One day, to honour his brother who had sacrificed so much, Albrecht Dürer drew his abused hands with palms together, thin fingers stretched upwards. He called his powerful drawing 'Hands', but all who saw it opened their hearts to his masterpiece and renamed it 'The praying hands'.

Look at your own hands

How wonderfully your hands are designed! Imagine having no thumb—how limited you would be. Or imagine having no fingernails to protect your fingers and add strength to them. Think of all the small jobs you are enabled to do by having fingernails.

Think how the joints enable you to flex, pick up and hold, caress, lift or pull.

Look at the patterns on the thumbs and fingers, which are uniquely yours. No one else in the world who has lived, lives or will live in the future has exactly the same pattern, which is why fingerprints are taken to prove our identity.

Look at the back of your hands: perhaps ageing spots are appearing or there are some scars from former injuries. There may even be signs of arthritis. Trace the course of the veins on your hand. They hold your lifeblood.

Perhaps you have a ring on your hand that signifies a relationship. I remember, after my mother died, we arranged to have her open coffin at her home on the day before her funeral. As my brothers and I stood around it, I suggested that we focus on her folded hands, still bearing her wedding ring, and reflect on all that those hands had done for us, her children and her grandchildren, over the years. It was very moving.

Look again at your hands.

They are hands that can express love and care and blessing.
They can receive the bread and wine of Holy Communion.
They are used for survival—feeding, drinking, clothing, washing, protecting.
Hands are for work, whatever form that takes.
They are used for communication and gesture.
You can use them for being creative and for making things.
They are capable of wounding but also of comforting.
They can be clenched in anger, restless with anxiety or open in generosity.
They can be strong or gentle.
They can be laid on someone in an act of prayer for healing.

What will you choose to use them for?
Clench your fists hard and then slowly uncurl the fingers until your hands are relaxed and open. Experience the contrast between closure and receptivity, between grasping and letting go.
Is there any experience or relationship in your life that needs releasing? If you identify one, you can use your hands as a symbol of moving from one attitude, which is closed and defensive, to another that is generous, open and life-giving.

For reflection
Can a mother forget the baby at her breast
and have no compassion on the child she has borne?
Though she may forget, I will not forget you.
See, I have engraved you on the palms of my hands.
(Isaiah 49:15–16)

Prayer

Lord, I bless you for the gift of my hands.
May they be used to worship you
and to love and serve others.
Lord, open my hands
and I shall show your generosity. Amen

The road travelled

You will need at least two hours for this exercise. You will need pens (preferably in three colours), a pencil, sticky tape and several sheets of blank A4 paper (one for each decade of your life plus two extra sheets).

Like a babbling stream that never stops flowing, life moves on. Each day differs from the next, even if only in a minor way. So many influences are brought to bear on us, especially in our formative childhood years. Like actors on a stage, people have entered our life and people have exited, but each one has left his or her own mark on us, whether positive or negative.

Over the years, we have developed physically and mentally, emotionally and spiritually. But I would guess it is rare that we take time to stop, look back and reflect on the way we have come, or to think about what we would like to build into the years that lie ahead, whether they are few or many. This exercise offers an opportunity to do just that.

Settle yourself at a table with your pens and paper.

Remind yourself that you are in God's presence and his Holy Spirit is your helper.

Pray for the grace to remember and accept whatever comes to your mind—the joys and the pains, the major events and the ordinary times, which are all part of the weaving of life.

There is no point in your life at which God has not known you and loved you.

Taking the first piece of paper and turning it so that it lies horizontally, give it the heading 'Years 0–10'. You are going to draw a line horizontally across the centre of the page, from one side to the other. Now make ten marks on the line, with roughly the same space between each mark, to indicate the years of this decade. If the space feels a bit cramped for writing on, you can use a page for each five years of your life.

Turn your piece of paper round so that it is vertical and write on it anything that you remember happening to you in each year (you can write either side of the line). There might be a house move, a brother or sister being born, a grandparent dying, going to school, friends you made— anything that comes to mind. When you have completed that page, take another sheet of paper and repeat the exercise for the next decade of your life, making sure that your line across the page is at the same height as the previous page, as you will eventually join them up to form one long horizontal line.

Continue the exercise for each decade of your life so far. When you have filled in all your years, take a break. Make yourself a drink, stretch your legs or put on a piece of music —whatever relaxes you.

Return to the pages and tape them together at the shorter sides so that a long line is formed—your river of life. Taking a different coloured pen, go back to the start and draw a line that will show the highs and the lows, letting it cross over your central line, sometimes above and sometimes beneath it, depending on what you have written about. This is the line of your emotions. To give you an example, my line would have dipped down when I was sent away to school and would have reached a high when I got married or the children were born.

You may like to take a third colour and mark the times when you were most aware of God in your life. You may be surprised to find that it corresponds to some of your low times. That is often because, when stripped of our self-sufficiency, we depend more on God's help.

As you grow older, you can record more years and add them on to your 'river'.

When you have finished mapping your life, lay it out in front of you and sense God's presence with you as you review it.

Some questions to ask yourself.
- What do I want to give thanks for?
- What do I want to ask forgiveness for?
- What do I want to put behind me?
- What lessons have I learnt along the way?
- What am I looking forward to?
- What would I like to develop in my ongoing journey of life?

Prayers

Lord, you are with us on our journey through life.
You are our redeemer, our helper and our guide,
the one through whom we gain strength
and from whom we learn to love.
When we get it wrong, forgive us;
when we are afraid, steady us;
when we are under pressure, calm us,
so that step by step we may become more truly ourselves—
the people you created us to be,
that we might live to your glory. Amen

For all that has been—Thanks!
To all that shall be—Yes! [1]

Blessing

At the end of most of Paul's letters is the greeting: 'The grace of the Lord Jesus be with you' or 'The grace of the Lord Jesus Christ be with your spirit' but in his second letter to the Corinthians he ends with a trinitarian blessing: 'May the grace of the Lord Jesus Christ, and the love of God, and the fellowship of the Holy Spirit be with you all' (2 Corinthians 13:14, NIV). That is the theme that I have chosen to bring this book to a close.

Part 1: The grace of the Lord Jesus Christ

What is meant by the word 'grace'? The dictionary defines it as elegance, beauty of movement, or goodwill (for example, being granted 'a grace and favour house' by the Queen); doing something with 'good grace' means doing it cheerfully and willingly. I don't know that I was given the name for this reason, but my name, Ann, means 'grace', as do Anna and Hannah.

In spiritual terms, God's grace is his generosity shown to us, although we have done absolutely nothing to deserve it.

The world is filled with God's grace. He gives us a beautiful planet to live on which is sustained by his faithfulness, the sun for energy and warmth and light, water to drink, food to eat, abundance of seed and blossom and fruit, a carefully designed body, the day in which to be active and the night in which to rest, and the capacity to be relational beings who can give and receive love. Above all, he gave us Jesus.

We read at the start of John's Gospel, 'The Word [that is, Jesus] became flesh and lived among us, and we [his disciples] have seen his glory, the glory as of a father's only son, full of grace and truth. (John 1:14). John also wrote, 'From his fullness we have all received, grace upon grace. The law indeed was given through Moses; grace and truth came through Jesus Christ' (vv. 16–17).

Jesus was the grace of God in action. He showed us what the grace of God looks like in the way he cared for people, the way he listened to them, met their needs, forgave them, taught them the truth, served them and ultimately died for them and for us. It is fascinating to read through the Gospels finding examples of grace in Jesus' generosity and kindness, and truth in his teaching.

There is nothing we can do to make God love us more. There is nothing we can do to make God love us less.

Do we really believe that? It is pure grace.

One Old Testament image of grace and blessing is dew. Throughout the Psalms, dew represents blessing, a gift from God. Still today, on the first day of Passover, the traditional beginning of the dry season in Israel, the Jews pray for dew in the summer. Dew falls silently, mysteriously, everywhere. It is wet and refreshing. Have you ever walked barefoot in dew-covered grass? It is a delightful experience on a warm morning. In the late summer and early autumn there are heavy morning dews and spiders' webs are made visible as they lie on the grass or are strung in between a framework such as branches or railings.

So it is with God's grace. It is for everyone. It is abundant, refreshing, transforming. It falls on everyone, the faithful and the unfaithful, the wise and the foolish. All we are asked to do is to receive it, just as the grass receives the dew. We can do nothing to earn it, but we can learn to live in the experience of God's grace; we can allow it to form our attitudes and behaviour and let its generosity rub off on us, so that we in turn show generosity and grace to others.

The grace of Jesus is seen supremely on the cross. With outstretched arms, it is as if he says, 'This is what I mean when I say I love you'.

For reflection
In the morning there was a layer of dew around the camp. When the layer of dew lifted, there on the surface of the wilderness was a fine flaky substance, as fine as frost on the ground. When the Israelites saw it, they said to one another, 'What is it?' For they did not know what it was. Moses said to them, 'It is the bread that the Lord has given you to eat.' (Exodus 16:13–15)

Jesus said, 'I am the bread of life. Your ancestors ate the manna in the wilderness, and they died. This is the bread that comes down from heaven, so that one may eat of it and not die. I am the living bread that came down from heaven. Whoever eats of this bread will live for ever; and the bread that I will give for the life of the world is my flesh.' (John 6:48–51)

A poem

Given so much,
What have I done to deserve it?
Nothing.
Absolutely nothing.

No wonder my heart
Dances[1]

An exercise

For this reflection you will need a glass tumbler, a bowl and a jug that holds more water than the tumbler.

I suggest that you sit in front of the bowl and stand the glass inside it. Have the jug of water ready next to it.

Become aware of how you are feeling at this moment. What is occupying your mind? What might be causing you concern? How is your health? What level would you say your energy is at?

Can you think of an image that might describe your current situation—a tangled ball of thread, a snail with its horns drawn in, a pile of clutter, a landscape? You will come up with your own image.

How does what you feel affect you physically, mentally, emotionally and spiritually?

If we are overloaded, depressed, lonely or just not feeling well, we can lose sight of the blessings that we have in our life.

I suggest that you pour a little water into your glass and, as you do so, name one blessing that is yours. It may be to do with God, family, friends, a pet animal, a work situation, your garden, a church—anything that encourages you, is tender and loving, offers solidarity, makes you feel safe or opens up new possibilities.

Keep pouring water into your glass, a little at a time, and continue to name any blessings that you can think of. Don't worry if the water reaches the top of the glass; continue pouring until the water overflows into the bowl.

When you feel that, for now, you have exhausted all the blessings that come to mind, sit back and look at the water and think of all that it represents.

Instead of filling the glass, you may like to imagine yourself being filled with the blessings you have named until they overflow and engulf you.

Jesus said, 'I came that they may have life, and have it abundantly' (John 10:10).

Let your experience lead you into thankfulness and praise.

Leave the glass of water and the bowl around for a while as a reminder of the many blessings in your life.

Part 2: The love of God

The sun, the sponge and the sea are three images that come to mind when I think about the love of God.

The sun

The sun is always shining, but our side of the planet may have turned away from it, so that it is visible on the other side of the earth, while we are in darkness. Even when we are in daylight, clouds may pass in front of the sun or cover the sky all day. But we have only to take off in a plane to realise that we are soon through the cloud cover, to emerge where the sun is shining in all its glory.

God's love is like the sun. It is always there but, in difficult circumstances or stressful relationships, preoccupations, illness or depression, we can experience a sense of God's absence, as if clouds have blocked out the sun.

His love is unconditional but to experience it we have to come into its light, allowing ourselves to be open to his loving presence.

What holds us back?

1. Unworthiness: The love we experience in our lives may be conditional; we often measure God's love in terms of other people's love, which we may feel we need to earn. We can confuse God's unconditional love with approval. God does not say, 'I'll love you if…' God never gives up loving us, even though he may be saddened by what we do or say. In Jesus' story of the prodigal son (Luke 15:11–32), the father who represents God the Father shows love that is freeing, yearning, forgiving and restoring.
2. False images of God: If we are afraid of God, we cannot love God or receive his love. Love means intimacy, closeness and a deep sense of safety, but all those things are impossible as long as there is fear. Fear creates suspicion, distance and insecurity. If, in our minds, God demands 100 per cent effort from us, this will lead to a constant sense of failure on our part, which works against intimacy.
3. The inability to accept and love ourselves: We are a mixture of positives and negatives, good and bad, faith and doubt—and always will be. God accepts us as we are, not as we would like to be.

4. Too many unanswered questions and perplexities: It is through faith that we experience love first and foremost, rather than by demanding proof or watertight answers (although, of course, such things have their place in the Christian life).

Henri Nouwen writes:

For most of my life I have struggled to find God, to know God, to love God. I have tried hard to follow the guidelines of the spiritual life—pray, work for others, read the Scriptures and avoid many of the temptations to dissipate myself. I have failed many times but always tried again, even when I was close to despair. Now I wonder whether I have sufficiently realised that during all this time God has been trying to find me, to know me, and to love me. The question is not 'How can I find God?' but 'How can I let myself be found by Him?' The question is not 'How can I know God?' but 'How am I to let myself be known by God?' And finally, the question is not 'How am I to love God?' but 'How am I to let myself be loved by God?' God is looking into the distance for me, as the father looked for the prodigal son, trying to find me, and longing to bring me home.[2]

The sponge

God desires intimacy. He is both infinite and intimate. His majesty and mystery leave us reeling, awed and amazed. As the psalmist wrote, 'O Lord, our Sovereign, how majestic is your name in all the earth! ... When I look at your heavens, the work of your fingers, the moon and the stars that you have established; what are human beings that you are mindful of them, mortals that you care for them?' (Psalm 8:1, 3–4). But the truth is that, as well as being so far beyond us, he is also intimate and close to us.

In Isaiah 40, both facets of God are poetically described. Among the examples of his majesty and sovereignty is this intimate picture of God as a shepherd: 'He will feed his flock like a shepherd; he will gather the lambs in his arms, and carry them in his bosom, and gently lead the mother sheep' (v. 11).

Jesus prayed to his Father and said, 'I made your name known to them, and I will make it known, so that the love with which you have loved me may be in them, and I in them' (John 17:26). We have the promise of Christ in us, nothing less. This is his prayer.

Drop a bath sponge or washing-up sponge into a bowl of water. It will absorb the water so that the sponge will be in the water and the water will be in the sponge. This is the intimacy that Christ offers us. He desires to be in us and for us to be in him.

The sea

Imagine going down to the sea's edge on a summer day, dressed for swimming. You stand in the shallows and let the water wash over your feet on the incoming tide, feeling the undertow as each wave recedes. You could stay and paddle or you could begin to walk out a little further until the water is up to your knees; a little further on and the water is up to your chest, but your feet are still on the ground; a few more steps and you can only stand on tiptoe. Then you decide to launch yourself into the sea, feet off the ground, letting the gentle waves carry you; you begin to swim or turn on to your back to float, looking up to the sky, abandoning yourself to the sea and its rocking motion.

The love of God is like the sea, and I can choose simply to paddle in its shallows, not daring to believe that he really loves me with all my inadequacies and selfishness. To truly experience his love, though, I need to take my feet off the ground and, in faith and trust, abandon myself to the sea of his love; to float and rest in God, letting him take me where he will.

For reflection

O the deep, deep love of Jesus!
Vast, unmeasured, boundless, free!
Rolling as a mighty ocean
In its fullness over me.
Underneath me, all around me,
Is the current of thy love;
Leading onward; leading homeward,
To my glorious rest above.

O the deep, deep love of Jesus!
Love of every love the best;
'Tis an ocean vast of blessing,
'Tis a haven sweet of rest.
O the deep, deep love of Jesus
'Tis a heaven of heavens to me
And it lifts me up to glory,
For it lifts me up to thee.[3]

Part 3: The fellowship of the Holy Spirit

The concept of the Trinity is a difficult one for our finite minds to grasp. It is a communion of three in one: Father, Son and Holy Spirit are separate and distinct but, at the same time, they are interdependent and equal. They live in one another and are part of each other, yet they still have separate identities. There is no Father-like being on his own, and no Son-like being on his own. The Father is only the Father because of the Son, and the Son is only the Son in relation to the Father. The Spirit is a full member of the Godhead and shares the same relationship with the other two persons of the Trinity as they share with the Spirit.

The Spirit was promised by Jesus. He said that he would ask the Father to send the Spirit into the world, and especially into the hearts of men and women who put their faith in God.

The Holy Spirit has identifiable roles:

- He is God's agent, God's transmitter. When music is performed, we hear it and enter into the experience of it through the sound waves. The Holy Spirit is like those sound waves, enabling us to receive God's revelation.
- He is the one who opens our eyes and makes Jesus known. He is the bringer of truth. His work is to convict of sin those who are opposed to Christ and to convince those who live in him of the truth. He is also the one who moves us to respond.
- He is God's comforter in the true meaning of the word, which is to 'give strength'.
- The Hebrew word for the Spirit is *ruach*, meaning 'wind'. The wind can be refreshing but it can also be disturbing, as

you will know if you have ever sat by an open window on a gusty day, with a pile of papers in front of you. I remember being at an all-age service on Pentecost Sunday. Each member of the congregation was given a piece of paper out of which we had to tear the rough shape of a human figure. The figures were then put in a pile at the front of the church, where they lay inactive. Then a leaf blower was directed on to them and the figures fluttered in the wind and were scattered around the church. It was a graphic teaching aid to show the effects of the Spirit's activity in our lives, which can't be predetermined or controlled. Jesus said, 'The wind blows wherever it pleases. You hear its sound, but you cannot tell where it comes from or where it is going. So it is with everyone born of the Spirit' (John 3:8).

Wind can also be a gentle breeze, the kind that refreshes on a hot day. The Holy Spirit, the agent of God, not only disturbs and motivates us but can also bring peace and restfulness. It is in quietness that we so often encounter God and are drawn into wonder and worship. From that still, deep God-space within us, we are asked to live out God's good news in the world.

• The Holy Spirit is our companion, as close to us as our own breath. Just as God breathed life into Adam, so Jesus breathes the life of God into us, as he did to his disciples. We read in John 20:21–22, 'Jesus said, "... As the Father has sent me, I am sending you." And with that he breathed on them and said, "Receive the Holy Spirit"' (NIV).

The Greek word for spirit is *pneuma*, which means 'breath'. Breath is essential for life; the Spirit of God is like our breath. It is the Holy Spirit of God who prays in us, reveals truth to us, makes us aware of God's love,

236

empowers us and heals us. We have nothing to offer the world in terms of the gospel if we are not inhabited and empowered by the Holy Spirit. We don't have to be anything special, just ourselves, but open to the influence of the Holy Spirit.

Moving deeper into the experience of the fellowship of the Holy Spirit means being open to receive, to hear, to discern, to be alert and sensitive, not relying solely on our common sense, to be disturbed and challenged, motivated to worship and to service.

For reflection
Read John 14:15–21 for the promise of the Holy Spirit; John 14:25–27 and 16:5–15 for the work of the Holy Spirit; Acts 2:1–21 and Romans 8:26–27 for the action of the Holy Spirit; and Romans 8:1–17 for a description of life in the Spirit.

Prayers

Spirit of truth
whom the world can never grasp,
touch our hearts
with the shock of your coming;
fill us with desire
for your disturbing peace;
and fire us with longing
to speak your uncontainable word
through Jesus Christ. Amen[4]

Come, Holy Spirit,
reveal to us the truth of God.

Come, Holy Spirit,
breathe Christ's life into us.

Come, Holy Spirit,
inflame our hearts with love.

Come, Holy Spirit,
pray through us to the Father.

Come, Holy Spirit,
energise us in God's service;

so may we bring glory to God
the Father, Son and Holy Spirit. Amen

Questions to ask
- In what ways have you known the Holy Spirit's action in your life?
- How has he guided you?
- Is there anything that he has convicted you about?
- What has he taught you about God?
- What has he reminded you about?
- How has he enabled you to worship God?
- How has he disturbed your life?
- How has he comforted you?

A prayer

May the grace of our Lord Jesus Christ, the love of God and the fellowship of the Holy Spirit be with us ever more. Amen

Notes

Ways into prayer

1   Lao-Tzu, *The Book of the Way*, trans. John Legge.

The God who comes

1   Bernard of Clairvaux (1090–1153), quoted in *They Laid Him in a Manger*, trans. David Smith (New City, 1990).

2   Richard Crashaw (1612–49), 'A hymn of the nativity'.

3   Gwylim R. Jones, translated into English for *A Welsh Pilgrims' Manual*, Brendan O'Malley (Gomer Press, 1989).

4   Evelyn Underhill, *An Anthology of the Love of God* (Mowbray, 1953), p. 54.

5   Michel Quoist, *Prayers of Life* (Logos Books, 1971), p. 14.

6   Maria Boulding, *The Coming of God* (SPCK, 1982), p. 66.

7   Hugh St Victor (c. 1078–1141).

8   William Young Fullerton, 'I cannot tell' (1929).

Winter

1   Percy Bysshe Shelley, 'Ode to the west wind' (1820).

2   Paula Gooder, *The Meaning is in the Waiting* (Canterbury Press, 2008).

3   Jean Vanier, *The Broken Body: Journey to wholeness* (DLT, 1988), p. 63.

A time to be born

1   Anon, in Janet Morley (ed.), *Bread of Tomorrow* (SPCK/Christian Aid, 1992), p. 50.

2   Pope Leo the Great (c.400–461), quoted in Smith (trans.), *They Laid Him in a Manger*.

3   Phillips Brooks, 'O little town of Bethlehem' (1867).

The magi came bearing gifts

1   Kate Compston, quoted in *Bread of Tomorrow*, p.58.

Desert encounters: Lent

1   One of the 'Psalms for life and peace' that first appeared in *Páginas* 1987, reprinted in *Latinamerica Press*, 5 November 1987.

2   Richard Rohr, *Everything Belongs* (Crossroad, 1999), p. 170.

Spring

1   Robert Frost, 'Two tramps in mud time', *Selected Poems* (Penguin, 1967), p. 165.

2   A.E. Housman, 'Loveliest of trees', *The New Dragon Book of Verse* (Oxford Univeristy Press, 1977), p. 9.

Parting gifts

1   From *Holy Week, Easter: Services and Prayers* (CHP, 1984), p. 194.

A time to die

1   Isaac Watts, 'When I survey the wondrous cross' (1707).

Early in the morning

1   Nicola Slee, *Easter Garden* (Fount, 1990), p. 189.

Meeting the risen Jesus

1   *Sacred Space: The Prayer Book 2007* (Veritas), p. 152.

2   St Augustine of Hippo (354–430), in Angela Ashwin, *The Book of a Thousand Prayers* (Marshall Pickering, 1996), p. 18.

Thomas

1   Janet Morley, *All Desires Known* (SPCK, 1992), p. 15.

Summer

1   Muriel Stuart, 'The seed shop', *The Golden Treasury of Poetry* (Collins, 1969), p. 257.

2   John Powell, *Through Seasons of the Heart* (Fount, 1989), p. 373.

He restores my soul

1   George Appleton, taken from *The Lion Prayer Collection*, compiled by Mary Batchelor (Lion Hudson, 2001)

Autumn

1   From Joyce Rupp, *May I Have This Dance?* (Ave Maria Press, 1992).

2   John O'Donohue, *Anam Cara* (Bantam, 1997).

3   From *Woman's Prayer Companion* (Carmelites of Indianapolis, 1993), quoted in Ashwin, *The Book of a Thousand Prayers*, p. 391.

Open hands

1   R.S. Thomas, 'The hand', *Collected Poems of R.S. Thomas* (JM Dent, 1993), p. 264.

The road travelled

1   Dag Hammarskjold, *Markings* (Faber and Faber, 1964), p. 87.

Blessing

1   Ann Lewin, 'Thanksgiving', *Watching for the Kingfisher* (Canterbury Press, 2009).

2   Henri Nouwen, *The Return of the Prodigal Son* (DLT, 1992).

3   Samuel Trevor Francis, 'O the deep, deep love of Jesus' (1875).

4   Morley, *All Desires Known*, p. 17.